The
Economist
PUBLICATIONS

Pocket Taxpayer

The
Economist

PUBLICATIONS

Pocket Taxpayer

HODDER AND STOUGHTON
LONDON SYDNEY AUCKLAND TORONTO

British Library Cataloguing in Publication Data

Sabine, B. E. V.
   Economist pocket taxpayer.
   1. Taxation — Great Britain — Dictionaries
   I. Title
336.2'00941 HJ2608

   ISBN 0-340-41480-4

Jacket by Rufus Segar
Illustrations by Rufus Segar

Set in Great Britain for Hodder and Stoughton Educational,
a division of Hodder and Stoughton Ltd.
Mill Road, Dunton Green, Sevenoaks, Kent,
by Paston Press, Loddon, Norfolk.

Printed by Hollen St. Press, Slough

Contents

Preface

The *Pocket Taxpayer* is a new method of presenting the basic principles of British taxation as they affect the individual taxpayer who is an employee; that is, the person who pays most, if not all, his tax under Schedule E by means of weekly or monthly deductions under the Pay As You Earn (PAYE) system. It covers all the legislation up to and including the Finance Act, 1986, in outline.

Inevitably that legislation cannot be covered in detail for it has now reached the formidable total of over a million words, quite apart from the cases to elucidate the complexity of the Taxes Acts pronounced on by the Courts.

But the format of using an alphabetical order enables any taxpayer to refer to the book for a speedy explanation of any point of interest or the answer to any particular problem in the first instance.

It may well be that in many cases the information provided will be adequate and the book will have then served its purpose. In some cases, however, the immediate reply will only have indicated that a problem exists and, briefly, its nature and context. It will then be essential to take professional advice. The book is a guide only: it is not a substitute for fiscal expertise.

For the last claim which could be made for income tax is simplicity. The reasons are not far to seek. It was first imposed in 1799 and, apart from the period when it was abolished from 1816 to 1842, it has been annually added to, subtracted from and generally amended for the past century and a quarter. The schedular division, for example, and the principle of deduction of tax at source, keystones of the British tax system, originated in 1803 and were retained in the reintroduction of income tax by Peel in 1842, the Income Tax Act of that year being a virtual reprint of that of 1802.

So the good ship income tax has sailed on through the storm of consolidation (1918 and 1970), a miscellaneous series of tempests in the shape of Committees and Royal Commissions, gradually accumulating a collection of barnacles. It has also gradually become more complex. There are many reasons for this: but the two principal influences have been the growing and parallel complexity of economic organisations with which fiscal legislation has had to keep pace; and the rise of avoidance, fuelled by high rates of tax. Avoidance breeds avoidance legislation. This in turn breeds more sophisticated planning so that ever more detailed legislation is needed for countermeasure.

It might be thought that this process would only affect business and corporate taxation. The truth is, however, that personal taxation has become almost equally elaborate. The days when it was simply a question of applying allowances to gross salary or wages have been overlaid by the PAYE system which, while the tax deducted needs little adjustment in the majority of cases, can create administrative problems. There is also a whole new code of benefits to be dealt with, share incentive schemes, deductions for business enterprise schemes, for retirement annuities, to name only a few of the modern developments affecting Schedule E; and although the *Pocket Taxpayer* does not pretend to show how this maze was created, it does provide, as already suggested, a guide through it.

NOTE: Cross-references are denoted by small capitals, and a list of the Board of Inland Revenue's publications has been included at the end of the book.

I should like to thank all those who have helped me to see the book through to completion, the editors at The Economist Publications and colleagues and secretaries at Deloitte, Haskins and Sells, especially Gary Hull ATII, who did much preliminary vetting for me; but I have to accept the overall responsibility.

Basil Sabine OBE MA FTII
Mottram-in-Longdendale
Cheshire.
Christmas 1986

A

Accommodation. See ANNUAL VALUE.

Accountant. The term is a general one, but is usually taken to mean a person who is professionally qualified, that is, a member or fellow of the Society of Chartered Accountants (ACA or FCA). There are several such societies all implying certain expertise but there is nothing to prevent anyone professing to be an accountant, so before any consultation it is as well to be satisfied about qualifications.

Professional fees are normally assessable under Schedule D, Case II (professions or vocations). They may be categorised as follows.

(a) Fees *paid* for completion of Schedule E return are not allowable, falling under the strict rule of not wholly, exclusively and necessarily incurred in the performance of the duties. But then the difference between the rules of Schedule D (trades) and Schedule E (employments) is unfair, cynically referred to as pay as you like and pay as you earn. Also not allowable are the fees for dealing with an investigation case regardless of the outcome.

(b) Fees *received* from holding an office and fees *paid* for preparing accounts and dealing with Schedule D computations are strictly assessable under Schedule E, for example, when an accountant is auditor of a limited company appointed under the Companies Act. See also TAX ACCOUNTANT.

Accounts year basis of assessment. One of the bases of Schedule E assessment. It simply means that the taxpayer is assessed on the figure of emoluments debited in the accounts for the year ending within the income tax year. If, for example, emoluments debited in the accounts to December 31, 1986, were £30,000 the amount assessed for 1986/87 would be the same. See also EARNINGS BASIS, RECEIPTS BASIS.

Accrued income scheme. One of the most complicated pieces of legislation in recent years. It is covered by the Finance Act, 1985, Sections 73–77 and Schedules 22 and 23, which ensure that accrued interest is taxed as income. See also BONDWASHING.

Accumulation and maintenance settlement. A settlement in which trustees manage capital on behalf of a beneficiary up to the age of 25. They can dispose of the increase, either by saving it up for him (in other words, accumulating) or by spending it for him if this seems desirable. For INHERITANCE TAX purposes, this form of settlement is especially favoured, provided certain stringent conditions are met. The most important of these is that a beneficiary *must* be entitled to receive income (though not necessarily capital) not later than age 25.

Acquisition. A technical term used in relation to:

(a) CAPITAL GAINS TAX to identify when an asset is acquired by the transferee and disposed of by the transferor. This date is normally the date of the contract (not of completion), unless the contract is conditional, when it is the date the condition is satisfied. See DISPOSAL.

(b) Schedule E, where a charge arises on a notional loan for employee shareholdings whether by allotment or assignment.

Additional personal allowance. (APA). See ALLOWANCES (c).

Additional rate. The tax charge additional to the basic and higher rates on:

(a) the investment income of an individual (abolished for the year 1984/85 and hereafter);

(b) the income of a DISCRETIONARY TRUST.

Age allowance. (AA). See MARRIAGE.

Age of majority. Now attained at the age of 18 (Family Law Reform Act, 1969).

Agency, worker supplied by. The services of a worker, contracted to an agency, performed for one of the agency's clients are treated for income tax purposes as if they were the duties of an employment held by that worker; he is, therefore, assessable under Schedule E. This legislation, however, is not taken to apply to actors, entertainers, or models.

Agent for taxpayer. The definition of a person as an agent stems from a relationship between two persons: the first expressly or impliedly consents that the second should act on his behalf: and the agent similarly consents to represent the first or so to act. Note that a taxpayer cannot hold his agent responsible for providing incorrect information on his tax affairs to the Inland Revenue.

Aggregation. The treatment of a married woman's income as that of her husband where it is income for a year of assessment or any part of a year of assessment beginning on April 6 during which she is living with her husband. It does not apply to a wife's earnings where an election has been made for SEPARATE ASSESSMENT or WIFE'S EARNINGS ELECTION, or in the year of marriage.

Alimony. See MAINTENANCE.

Allowances. There are several personal allowances or reliefs available to a taxpayer on the basis of status, whether single or married, and for dependants. For married allowance see HUSBAND AND WIFE. The other allowances which are deductible from income are as follows.

(a) *Single allowance*: the tax threshold available to all.

(b) *Housekeeper allowance*: available for widows and widowers for a resident housekeeper – rarely claimed in practice.

(c) *Additional personal allowance*: available for widows, widowers and single taxpayers for a dependent child or children and where the wife is incapacitated and the children are at home. It brings the single allowance up to the quantum of the married allowance.

(d) *Dependent relative allowance*: available for a taxpayer who maintains an incapacitated relative of his or his wife's mother (whether or not incapacitated) who is a widow or living apart from her husband. The allowance granted to a woman claimant other than a wife is greater than that for other taxpayers – currently £145 and £100 respectively. Note also that if the income of the dependent relative is more than the BASIC RETIREMENT PENSION, the allowance is reduced by the amount of that excess. Where the claimant contributes to a relative who is not living with him less than £75 annually, relief is given concessionally on the amount paid. In practice a contribution of more than £75 will attract the full relief. The figure of £75 is the current (1986) limit.

(e) *Allowance for the service of a daughter or a son*: An individual who, because of old age or infirmity, relies on the services of a son or daughter living with or maintained by him is entitled to an allowance.

Since 1980 allowances have been indexed and, apart from 1981/82, have risen annually by reference to the increase in the retail prices index. See also BLIND PERSON'S ALLOWANCE, LIFE ASSURANCE RELIEF, LORRY DRIVER.

Annual exemption. The two capital taxes – that is, INHERITANCE TAX (formerly capital transfer tax) and CAPITAL GAINS TAX – both have thresholds; and both these thresholds are currently indexed.

(a) *Inheritance (capital transfer) tax*: The annual amount of chargeable transfers in which IHT/CTT is not payable (usually £3,000). Any missed amount in one year can be carried forward for relief in the following year only, provided that the full annual exemption for the later year is taken up first. Note also that the first step in the IHT scale is taxed at a zero rate, and so effectively is exempt from tax. With effect from March 18, 1986, this was set at £71,000 and may be indexed annually by reference to the retail prices index.

(b) *Capital gains tax*: The annual amount of chargeable gains less allowable losses which is exempted from CGT. For 1986/87 it was fixed at £6,300 and may be indexed annually by reference to the retail prices index.

Annual payment. A transfer of income which is deemed to have paid tax. It includes an ANNUITY. The word 'annual' is important and means that the payment must have the quality of being recurrent or capable of being recurrent.

Annual value (including accommodation).

(a) When accommodation is provided by an employer to a director or higher paid employee, the assessable benefit is measured by taking the rent which might reasonably be expected to be obtained, taking one year with another, if the tenant paid all the usual tenant's burdens and the landlord undertook to bear all the usual landlord's burdens to maintain the property in a state fit to command that rent. It is otherwise known as the *rack rental value* and was the basis for the old Schedule A assessment.

(b) The annual value concept was also applied to cars assessable as a benefit but from 1981/82 the charge has been based on the scale charge (see CAR).

(c) For other assets, it is normally taken as 20 per cent of the market value of the asset when made available to the employee.

Annuity. The ANNUAL PAYMENT of a certain sum of money. It can include a voluntary annuity or one which is capable of being discontinued.

Annuities may be paid free of tax, in which case special calculations are necessary to arrive at the *gross equivalent* to determine any higher rate or additional tax that may be due.

Appeals. See OBJECTIONS AND APPEALS.

Approved pension schemes. Pension and similar schemes set up by an employer for the benefit of his employees and approved by the Superannuation Funds Office are exempt from tax on income and capital gains. The contributions to such a fund by the employer and the employee are deductible for tax purposes. Schemes which have been established by statute receive automatic approval. See RETIREMENT.

Approved share option schemes. This is one of several share schemes (see also SHARE INCENTIVE SCHEMES and PROFIT SHARING SCHEMES) and even this must be considered in two parts.

(a) Up to 1966 if a director or employee of a company acquired an enforceable right to buy shares in a company he was regarded as assessable on the value of that right the day it was granted less any sum paid for it. The law was then changed to delay the tax chargeable until the exercise of the option.

In 1980, however, the concept of an approved savings related share option was reintroduced. An individual can now obtain a right to acquire at a modest level shares in a company by reason of his employment as a director or employee of that company without attracting income tax either on the acquisition of that option or on its exercise; or in respect of any increase in the value of the shares. The scheme requires that he contributes regularly to a SAYE scheme (as operated by a building society through his employer) for five years.

(b) A different form of approved share option was introduced in 1984. In contrast to the 1980 scheme, there is no requirement that the scheme must be linked with savings, nor need all employees participate on equal terms: it can be limited to a selected group. The value of the options granted may be as much as £100,000 or four times the employee's remuneration. A principal company may extend it to other companies which it controls and may operate it in conjunction with other share schemes.

The Board of Inland Revenue must approve all such schemes and they are to be submitted to Inland Revenue, Technical Division (Employee Share Schemes) New Wing, Somerset House, Strand, London, WC2.

Assessing district. A taxpayer may have sources of income arising in more than one tax district, but one district, usually that which deals with his principal source of income, will take responsibility for instructing the other district how the other sources of income are to be charged. It is to that district he makes his return and the Revenue refers to it as his *general claims district*.

Many Schedule E sources of income arising in London are dealt with in special districts known as LONDON PROVINCIAL DISTRICTS because they are in the provinces. If a personal interview is required, it is possible to have a file sent to the district most convenient for the taxpayer to get to. See also ENQUIRY OFFICES and DISTRICTS.

Assessment. Assessments to tax are generally made by the Inspector of Taxes, although certain categories of tax (for example, inheritance tax) are assessed formally by the Board of Inland Revenue. An assessment is based, if possible, on a completed RETURN of income, but the absence of such a return is no bar to an assessment; and the Inspector may make an assessment to the best of his judgement if dissatisfied with a return.

Schedule E assessments are not made annually unless there is a considerable difference between the tax chargeable and that deducted under the PAYE scheme; but an assessment will always be made on request.

Schedule D assessments are normally made automatically before the normal due date of payment of the tax and may be made in an estimated amount in the absence of a return.

Normally assessments may be made at any time not later than six years after the end of the year of assessment to which the assessment relates but this may be extended in certain circumstances. See FRAUD and WILFUL DEFAULT.

The Inspector can also make an additional assessment if he discovers that income has not been assessed. 'Discovers' has been held to mean has 'reason to believe', 'is satisfied' or 'comes to the conclusion on information before him'. See also DISCOVERY.

Assessment, notice of. May be issued at any time but until it is no legal liability for the tax charged can arise. A notice gives the amount of income assessed, details of the deductions granted, calculation of the tax payable, the time limit for appeal and the address of the Inspector responsible for the issue (it may have been prepared at a computer centre). The date of issue must also be shown since this sets the due date of payment and the period for appeal. As a notice of assessment is not invalidated by any technical error, it should not be ignored if, for example, a name is wrongly spelled or the income not correctly described.

Assets provided by employer. Where an asset – a house, for example – is placed at an employee's or his household's disposal, there is an assessment on the benefit. This is measured by the ANNUAL VALUE of the use of the asset plus the total cost of providing the benefit. For the calculation of annual value see ANNUAL VALUE as far as CARS and accommodation are concerned: for other assets the annual value is a percentage (before 1980, 10 per cent; currently 20 per cent) of the market value of the asset at the date when it was first provided by the employer as a benefit for the employee.

Note that the total cost of providing the asset does not include any rent or hire charge paid, or any of the costs of acquiring or producing it.

Assets transferred not at arm's length. Where an asset is transferred to an employee or to a member of his family or household not AT ARM'S LENGTH, the cost of the assessable benefit is deemed to be the MARKET VALUE of the asset at the time of transfer. However, an alternative method is used if it throws up a larger liability than taking market value. This treats the cost of the benefit as the market value of the asset when it first ranked as a benefit reduced by the amounts charged for its use. Any consideration given by the transferee must be deducted from the cost of the benefit. The balance remaining is the cash equivalent of the benefit. This second calculation is rare.

Where an asset is transferred by way of gift, capital gains tax is chargeable as if the asset had been sold at its open market value. This liability may be deferred (see HOLDOVER RELIEF).

At arm's length. The relationship between persons who bear no duty, obligation or relation to each other so that any transaction between them is on a wholly commercial basis. See MARKET VALUE.

Available accommodation. A significant factor in deciding whether, for tax purposes, a person is ORDINARILY RESIDENT in the UK. The Inland Revenue takes the view that a person has to have been in the UK for at least three years before being so regarded. Buying accommodation to use and occupy, however, can create this status earlier. However, if this residence is not used but rented out, without a period being set aside for the owner's occupation, or is let on short tenancies or is available for letting, it is not regarded as being available for use and status is not affected.

Avoidance. The process of so arranging tax affairs that the amount of tax legally due is less than would be payable by following the obvious or more usual course. It is lawful provided it involves no concealment of material facts.

Avoidance is as old as taxation itself and it was not long after the Courts were permitted to review the decisions of Commissioners in 1874 that they were called upon to pronounce on avoidance. There are three classic judicial dicta on avoidance, given here in chronological order.

(a) 'No man in this country is under the smallest obligation, moral or other, so to arrange his legal relations to his business or to his property as to enable the Inland Revenue to put the largest possible shovel into his stores. The Inland Revenue is not slow – and quite rightly – to take every advantage which is open to it under the taxing statutes for the purpose of depleting the taxpayer's pocket. And the taxpayer is, in like manner, entitled to be astute to prevent so far as he honestly can, the depletion of his means by the Inland Revenue.' Lord Clyde, *Ayrshire Pullman Motor Services and Ritchie v. IRC* (1929) 14 TC 754.

(b) 'The highest authorities have always recognised that the subject is entitled so to arrange his affairs as not to attract taxes imposed by the Crown, so far as he can do so within the law, and that he may legitimately claim the advantage of any express terms or of any omissions that he can find in his favour in taxing Acts. In doing so he neither comes under liability nor incurs blame.' Lord Sumner, *IRC v. Fisher's Executors* (1926) 10 TC 302.

(c) 'Every man is entitled, if he can, to order his affairs so that the tax attracted under the appropriate Act is less than it otherwise would be. If he succeeds in ordering them so as to secure this result, then however unappreciative the Commissioners of Inland Revenue or his fellow taxpayers may be of his ingenuity, he cannot be compelled to pay an increased tax.' Lord Tomlin, *IRC v. Duke of Westminster* (1936) 19 TC 490.

The spirit of these dicta was possibly watered down slightly during the Second World War. But it still remained true that taxpayers were entitled to use avoidance techniques and practitioners could hardly refuse to advise them, although they might do so with some reluctance.

But in the 1970s avoidance became an industry and eventually the Courts took the view that if there was a series of preconceived or preordained transactions that in reality formed part of a single composite transaction with no business purpose (though not necessarily no business effect) and if the whole and only purpose of the scheme was tax avoidance, then the Courts were entitled to look through the scheme to its logical end; and, although each step might be legally justified, if there was no commercial justification and the end was pure avoidance, the scheme failed.

This concept is still evolving and it is increasingly difficult for the practitioner to advise a client on planning which seems to contain elements of avoidance. In addition, there can be avoidance schemes so convoluted that the material and relevant facts become, possibly deliberately, almost impossible to unravel. In such circumstances, it could be said avoidance is shading off into EVASION. It is certainly true that the running battle between avoidance and legislation, which has created complex statutes, is far from over.

Audit, PAYE. There have always been audit staff from the Collector's office to look into the proper operation of the PAYE system ever since it was set up in 1943. But with the recent concentration of the Revenue on investigation, the activity of the PAYE Audit Section has increased considerably.

Its brief is firstly to see that the PAYE procedures are being properly operated: that tax is being deducted from all remuneration in accordance with each employee's code; and that the tax thus deducted is being fully accounted for to the Collector on the due date. It has the right to visit premises and inspect all the relevant documents.

Its main target is the payment of sums which could amount to remuneration in the form of expenses, wages to casual workers who may have other jobs and directors' receipts of all kinds.

It is important to remember, if the PAYE Audit Section announces that it wishes to inspect the records, to alert the firm's tax adviser so he can first review the operation of the system and check for any irregularities. When the actual investigation starts it may be too late for remedies and the result can be expensive in tax and penalties.

Awards.

(a) *Gallantry awards.* Up to 1980/81 the annuity and additional pension paid to a holder of the Victoria Cross and the annuity paid to the holder of the George Cross were exempt from tax. From 1980/81 the additional pension paid to the holder of the George Cross became exempt and also the annuities paid to holders of the Military Cross, the Distinguished Flying Cross, the Distinguished Conduct Medal, the Conspicuous Gallantry Medal, the Distinguished Service Medal, the Military Medal and the Distinguished Flying Medal.

(b) *Awards paid to employees* for suggestions are not taxed, provided the reward is appropriate to the suggestion and it comes within the usual duties of the person making the suggestion.

(c) Employers may enter into arrangements with the Revenue to meet the basic rate liability of employees on the grossed up value of *non-cash incentive prizes and awards* which are considered taxable. Valuation of the award depends on the way the scheme has been set up. Details of the arrangement are obtainable from Inland Revenue, Incentive Valuation Unit, 4th Floor, 27 Broadwick Street, London W1V 2AE.

B

Back duty. The strict definition is tax charged by the Revenue under a claim that such tax has been lost owing to a taxpayer's NEGLECT, WILFUL DEFAULT or FRAUD. Clearly, traders are more likely than employees to be the subject of enquiry, because employees have fewer opportunities for concealing income. The phrase is now slightly old-fashioned.

Balancing allowances and charges. An individual assessable under Schedule E may use for the purpose of that employment certain plant (for example, calculators or typewriters) or perhaps a car. He is entitled to a 25 per cent allowance on the written-down value of such assets annually (limited to £2,000 in the case of a car). When any asset comes to be sold, there will be a balancing allowance or balancing charge, depending on whether the sale price is smaller than or larger than the written-down value, on the deficiency or excess. If the sale price is more than the original cost, the profit element is ignored. Allowances may also be claimed by an employee where it is *necessary* for him to provide an asset (such as a car) to carry out the duties of his employment. See also CAPITAL ALLOWANCES.

Bank interest.

(a) *Paid*. See LOAN INTEREST.
(b) *Received*. Assessable on a previous year basis when the source is continuing. In the year when the income first arises, the assessment is on the full amount arising within that year. In the second year of assessment, the assessment is on the amount of income in that year of assessment. In the third year, the assessment will normally be on the same figure as that of the second year of assessment – that is, the previous year's figure. But the taxpayer has the option of claiming that the assessment for the third year should be adjusted to the actual amount received in that year when it is to his advantage. This claim must be made in writing at any time within six years of the end of the year of assessment.

With effect from April 6, 1985, interest paid by UK banks is normally paid under deduction of COMPOSITE RATE TAX and is treated as received by the depositor as already taxed at the BASIC RATE and included in his income on a current year basis. Any higher rate liability is assessed directly on the individual.

Basic rate. This is the rate of income tax charged on an individual's TOTAL INCOME up to the level at which the higher rates begin to apply. It is also the relevant rate for TAX CREDIT.

Basic retirement pension. The amount of the social security retirement pension (as defined) to which an individual is entitled by his own contributions. It is relevant in considering dependent relative allowance (see ALLOWANCES) since that is reduced by £1 for every £1 that the income of the dependent relative exceeds the pension limit.

Basis of assessment. Depends on the Schedule under which the income is to be assessed (see under SCHEDULE A etc; see also BANK INTEREST for previous year basis and ACCOUNTS YEAR BASIS OF ASSESSMENT). As far as Schedule E is concerned, the assessment used to be on a previous year basis until the arrival of PAYE. Clearly the new method of tax deduction made it necessary to change the basis of assessment; the remuneration payable for a year of assessment is now regarded as the assessable income of that year. When an assessment is on a previous year basis, as under SCHEDULE D, there are also special rules for the opening and closing years of assessment for a source of income.

Bed and breakfast. An avoidance device involving the selling of shares to create an allowable loss for capital gains tax and buying them back the following day. Although legislation to stop such transactions has often been threatened, they are still allowed. When the original INDEXATION provisions were introduced in 1982, these effectively excluded bed and breakfast operations; however, the provisions were amended in 1985 and the ability to carry these through was reinstated.

Beneficial loan arrangements. The term loan includes many forms of credit to an employee or a relative. A *relative* is specified as the spouse of the employee, or the parent, ancestor, lineal descendant, brother or sister (or their spouses) of the employee or employee's spouse. The recipient of such a loan is chargeable to tax on the difference between the interest paid and the official rate prescribed by the Treasury.

There is, however, no charge if:

(a) the difference is £200 (currently) or less;
(b) in a loan to a relative, he derived no benefit;
(c) the employer was acting as an individual and made the loan in the normal course of domestic, family or personal relationship;
(d) the interest is otherwise eligible for relief (see also BRIDGING LOANS);
(e) the amount advanced is for expenses necessarily incurred by an employee in performing the duties of his employment, provided that the maximum amount advanced at any one time is not more than £1,000 (currently) and that the advances are spent within six months and recorded.

Benefit. The application by a sporting club of the proceeds of a match, and often associated activities organised for the benefit of any of its players, usually a CRICKETER or a FOOTBALLER. A cricketer does not have an entitlement to a benefit written into his contract and it was decided by the Courts as long ago as 1927 that for that reason the receipts were not assessable. A footballer's benefit, however, is written into his contract and the receipts from it are regarded as assessable.

Benefits in kind. When employers began to provide benefits for their employees – about the time of the First World War – legislation was rather slow to catch up. By now, of course, there is a complex battery of provisions. The broad effect of these is that, where applicable, expenses payments and the value of benefits are assessed under Schedule E on the director or employee. He may then claim any expenses which are wholly, exclusively and necessarily incurred in the performance of his duties.

Some benefits are taxable on all employees but most of the legislation applies to directors and higher paid (currently £8,500) employees. This definition is fundamental to an understanding of taxable benefits since the provisions for valuing benefits vary according to the category into which an individual falls.

Broadly, for the director and higher paid employee, the general rule for liability is to assess the cash equivalent or cost of the benefit, that is, the actual expense incurred by the employer less any contribution from the employee. The basic rule for an employee who is earning *less* than £8,500 is that he is only liable on a benefit if it is convertible into money when the quantum of the assessment is the second-hand value.

Note that the £8,500 threshold includes the value of all benefits received as if the employee were higher paid and all expenses reimbursed before any deduction for those allowable. In addition, detailed returns of expenses are required by the Revenue on form P11D. See DISPENSATION.

As the legislation relating to benefits has now become extremely detailed, the various benefits are listed under their separate headings as follows.

ACCOMMODATION See ANNUAL VALUE
ASSETS   (a) PROVIDED BY EMPLOYER
                  (b) TRANSFERRED NOT AT ARM'S LENGTH
BENEFICIAL and BRIDGING LOAN ARRANGEMENTS
CANTEEN FACILITIES
CARS
CREDIT CARDS
ENTERTAINMENT
EXAMINATION EXPENDITURE
HOLIDAYS
LUNCHEON VOUCHERS
MEDICAL INSURANCE
NURSERY FACILITIES
PRIZE INCENTIVE SCHEMES
SCHOLARSHIPS   See EDUCATIONAL AND SCHOLARSHIP SCHEMES
SEMINARS and CONFERENCES
SUGGESTIONS SCHEMES PAYMENTS See AWARDS
TRANSPORT VOUCHERS
WELFARE, SPORTS and SOCIAL FACILITIES

Bereavement allowance. See HUSBAND AND WIFE.

BES, see BUSINESS EXPANSION SCHEME.

Black economy. Black is reckoned to be the colour of turpitude, so as black market became the description of buying and selling outside the law so the black economy is the fiscal phrase for dealing and the providing of services outside the codes of the Inland Revenue, Customs and Excise and the DHSS.

In the USA this is called the underground economy, and it is not easy to define with any accuracy. This is partly because of the shadowy – even shady – nature of the various enterprises involved. It may be said to comprise businesses which operate outside the normal economic structure – that is, businesses which would tend not to recognise National Insurance obligations, VAT or income tax. They would not necessarily be illegal, but some would be on the fringe of criminal or semi-criminal activities concerned with goods of dubious provenance and origin, and with pornography and drugs. See also GHOSTS and MOONLIGHTING.

Blind person. A person who is registered as a blind person under the National Assistance Act, 1948, is entitled to an additional allowance if single or if married, if either spouse is a blind person; where both husband and wife are blind the allowance is doubled. This allowance is on top of the normal single or married allowance. Before 1981/82 the amount of the relief was scaled down by the amount of any tax-free disability payments but since then the restriction has been abolished.

Board of Customs and Excise. When farming of taxes ended in 1671, the Customs Board, as it was then called, was reconstituted with seven Commissioners. Customs provided the mainstay of the national revenue throughout the 18th and 19th centuries; not until the beginning of this century did direct overtake indirect taxation. In 1862 it was suggested that Customs might be amalgamated with the Inland Revenue but eventually it was decided in 1909 to join Customs and Excise (previously under the care of the Board of Inland Revenue), just in time to deal with Blériot's pioneer flight across the Channel and the growing popularity of the motor car.

Since then the Board has coped successfully with Purchase Tax (1940) as well as concentrating on its best payers – spirits, sugar, tobacco, beer and hydrocarbon oils – with a steadily rising level of receipts. The final change was the introduction of value added tax in 1972 as an entirely new fiscal weapon, at a rate currently only 14 per cent below the basic rate of income tax. The Board of Customs and Excise is one of the two great fiscal Boards with which the Chancellor holds important consultations when preparing his annual Budget. See BOARD OF INLAND REVENUE.

Board of Inland Revenue. Originally called the Commissioners for the Affairs of the Taxes, they were rechristened the Commissioners of Stamps and Taxes and, by the Inland Revenue Board Act 1849, became the Board of Inland Revenue. They shed their excise powers in 1909 (see BOARD OF CUSTOMS AND EXCISE) and now consist of seven members appointed by the Queen under the authority of the 1890 Inland Revenue Regulation Act.

The Taxes Management Act, 1970, states: 'Income tax, corporation tax and capital gains tax shall be under the care and management of the Commissioners of Inland Revenue (in this Act referred to as the Board).' In the exercise of their duty they are subject to the direction and control of the Treasury. There is an elaborate network of administration based in SOMERSET HOUSE, but there has been, since 1976, a regional structure also. The average taxpayer is, of course, more familiar with the DISTRICT and the INSPECTOR OF TAXES. This is the second of the two great Boards on which the Chancellor relies for both forecasts and provision of revenue. There is an annual Board's Report.

Board's pamphlets. Explanatory pamphlets published by the Board of Inland Revenue. They set out the statutory practice on a large number of fiscal topics in simple language, although of course, such explanations cannot be more than the Board's interpretation. The first pamphlet was published in 1799 and was entitled, 'A Short and Easy Description of the Income and Property Act so as to made it understanded of the meanest intelligence'. Today the Board's titles are more diplomatic. They can all be obtained from DISTRICTS and the INLAND REVENUE'S PRESS OFFICE free of charge. See list of Revenue pamphlets on p. 116.

Bondwashing. An avoidance device which consists of the sale of securities, with interest accrued, not long before the interest becomes due. The vendor rebuys the securities ex-dividend and therefore effectively recovers the gross interest as capital. This device was put a stop to on February 27, 1986: it was mainly used by life assurance companies, investment and unit trusts and Lloyd's syndicates rather than by individuals.

Bonus. A bonus is almost always regarded as part of the recipient's remuneration (it is often calculated in relation to profit) and so assessable under Schedule E; the circumstances would have to be exceptional for this not to be so. When it is paid after the year end it is assessable in the year to which it relates, irrespective of the year of payment.

Bridging loan interest.
(a) Where an individual takes out a bridging loan, the Revenue allows the interest for the first year even when over the limit of interest on £30,000 currently, and will extend the relief by concession to two and even three years in exceptional circumstances.
(b) Where a bridging loan for house purchase is provided by an employer for a director or higher paid employee, no benefit arises subject normally to a time limit of one year, currently extended to two years. It can exceed £30,000.

BSS. See BUSINESS START-UP SCHEMES.

Building Society interest. The income tax liability of a building society (which is defined as one within the Building Societies Act, 1962) is covered by an 'arrangement' with the Board of Inland Revenue, which provides, *inter alia*, that the liability of its investors to income tax (but not to higher rate tax) is discharged by the building society. Banks, including National Savings Banks, are now covered by the same composite rate scheme.

(a) Building society interest *received*, therefore, is treated as free of tax – that is, it is treated as being a net amount received under deduction of tax at basic rate. The tax notionally deducted is not repayable but is allowed as a credit when the income is assessed at higher rates.

(b) Building society interest *paid* was at first available for relief simply because it had been paid to a building society. In 1969, however, relief was restricted to interest on a 'loan for the purchase or improvement of land'. Now, from 1974, relief is limited to interest on loans for the purchase or improvement of main residences and the total of loans is limited currently to interest on £30,000; no account, however, is taken of interest added to capital not over £1,000.

Business and professional books and publications. The Revenue will generally admit the expense of a Schedule E taxpayer in providing himself with books and publications which are wholly, exclusively and necessarily required for the purpose of his employment – for example, a journalist's reference books. Books have been held to be a suitable asset for CAPITAL ALLOWANCES when used to stock a barrister's library; there is no Schedule E case tested as yet.

Business entertainment. Entertainment, which includes hospitality of any kind provided by an individual or by a member of his staff, will not be allowed unless the expenditure relates to an OVERSEAS CUS-TOMER. However, if an employee's entertaining expenses satisfy the 'wholly, exclusively and necessarily' test and are specifically reimbursed, they would be allowable, but would, of course, be disallowed in computing the employer's tax liability. STAFF ENTERTAINING is allowed if reasonable. The same principle of disallowance applies to VAT.

Business Expansion Scheme (BES). The scheme was introduced in 1983 as a replacement for the BUSINESS START-UP SCHEME, and much of the detailed legislation is identical.

As far as individuals are concerned, the major feature is the ability to invest in eligible shares issued by qualifying companies from £500 for each company to £40,000 in aggregate annually. The amount invested ranks as a deduction from total income. To qualify an individual must be resident in the UK; he must subscribe for the shares on his own behalf; and he must not be CONNECTED WITH THE COMPANY at any time within the relevant period. There is an overriding condition that the shares issued and subscribed for must be for *bona fide* commercial reasons and not as part of a tax avoidance scheme.

The 1986 Finance Act has laid down that the first sales of shares thus subscribed for after March 18, 1986, shall not attract capital gains liability, but that the type of company eligible shall not be heavily asset-backed. Also excluded are ventures whose main purpose is to hold goods for investment, such as wines or antiques. Nevertheless, BES is a very attractive proposition for those individuals with a high top marginal rate of income tax.

Business property relief. An IHT/CTT relieving provision relating to the transfer of business property where the whole or part of the value transferred can be attributed to such property. The value transferred (a certain percentage) is calculated as a value on which no tax is chargeable.

Business Start-Up Scheme (BSS). The first scheme of relief for investment in corporate trade was the Business Start-Up Scheme introduced by the Finance Act, 1981. For shares issued after April 5, 1983, it has been replaced by the BUSINESS EXPANSION SCHEME, which virtually took over the BSS framework and is in effect a substitution for it, and in fact, since the legislation in the 1986 Finance Act, certainly has more liberal conditions including indefinite prolongation.

Business travel. A long established principle is that the expense of travelling to the place of employment is not allowable because it is not incurred in the performance of the duties, with the emphasis on 'in'; an exception can arise where an employee is required to work from his own house. When, however, travelling is part of an employee's duties – as it is for a representative – not only will the cost of travelling be allowed but hotel expenses as well.

When an employee is required to work away from his main base of employment, his travelling to the temporary place of employment is allowable. Employees in the construction and allied industries may be entitled to allowance for travel, subsistence and lodgings under a collectively negotiated Working Rule. The Revenue is usually prepared to accept, if the amounts are reasonable, that the actual expenses are broadly equivalent to the allowances. Note that once the need for a travelling expense has been proved, it does not have to be 'wholly and exclusively'; these second two, usually inevitable Schedule E adverbs do not appear in the relevant section of the Act. The Revenue has recently conceded that travel to home after a period on oil rigs can be allowed. See TRAVELLING EXPENSES. In practice, the Revenue relaxes rules in the following circumstances.

(a) If public transport is disrupted by industrial action, the employer can reimburse the cost of/or provide free of charge, suitable transport or overnight accommodation close to the workplace.

(b) A severely disabled person who is incapable of using public transport because of his disability may be provided with alternative means of transport or receive financial assistance with the cost of journeys between his home and place of employment.

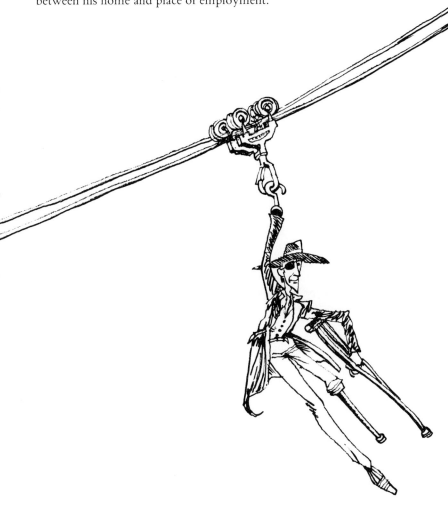

C

Calculators and so on, capital allowances for. Original legislation governing Schedule E expenses allowed the cost of travelling in the performance of the duties and of the upkeep of a horse. This is retained in current legislation, possibly for sentimental reasons. In 1925 the rules regarding wear and tear (CAPITAL ALLOWANCES) were extended to employments and provided the plant or machinery is necessarily required for the performance of the duties, allowances are due. This relief has become increasingly important. At one time a car was the main item for which the claim would be made (for details, see CAR). Now calculators, computers, word processors and typewriters attract relief, subject to the 'necessarily' proviso, noted above.

Canteens and dining rooms provided by employers. The benefit from these is not taxable provided it is available in one form or another to all staff; this applies to directors, higher and lower paid employees.

Capital allowances. As noted under the heading CALCULATORS AND SO ON, CAPITAL ALLOWANCES FOR, a wear and tear allowance, as it was then called, was extended in 1925 to employments and offices. This enabling provision was re-enacted in the Capital Allowances Act, 1968, which applied the rules relating to capital allowances for expenditure on plant and machinery to employments and offices so long as such expenditure was necessarily provided for in the performance of the duties of the employment.

An individual carrying on a TRADE or PROFESSION may also claim capital allowances as a deduction from his taxable profits.

The mechanics of the allowance are simply the deduction of 25 per cent of the written down value of the asset from total income. There can be an agreed restriction of the amount of the allowance to cover private use. For the position when the asset is sold, see BALANCING ALLOWANCES AND CHARGES.

Capital Gains Tax. This tax, which was introduced in 1965, is levied on CHARGEABLE GAINS accruing to any person in a year of assessment during any part of which he is RESIDENT or ORDINARILY RESIDENT in the UK.

The tax is levied on the disposal of assets and there are provisions relating to chargeable and exempt persons, chargeable and exempt assets, and chargeable occasions. The amount of the gain or loss is normally computed by subtracting the cost of the asset from the disposal of it, but there can be special rules for different situations. Only that part of a gain attributable to the period since April 5, 1965, is chargeable; and there has been an INDEXATION allowance since April 5, 1982. Disposals between husband and wife are ignored.

Capital gains tax is not chargeable on an individual's DEATH, although his assets are treated as passing at probate – that is, market – value. See also HOLDOVER RELIEF.

Capital receipt. This relates to a PROFIT SHARING SCHEME. A Schedule E charge can arise on an appropriate percentage of such a receipt if received before the release date to the extent that it constitutes income in the hands of the recipient for tax purposes; or it consists of a disposal of the participant's shares chargeable under Schedule E; or it consists of new shares. A rights adjustment, however, does not rank as a capital receipt. There is a *de minimis* limit of £10 under which no Schedule E charge arises.

A capital receipt may also represent a part DISPOSAL of an asset for CAPITAL GAINS TAX purposes, so giving rise to a chargeable gain or allowable loss; one example is a liquidation distribution.

Capital transfer tax. Capital transfer tax, which in 1975 replaced the estate duty of 1894, was a tax on all gratuitous transfers of capital whether they occurred during a lifetime or at death. It came into effect from March 26, 1974, for gifts and March 12, 1975, for death. There were two rates, the higher applying to transfers at death or within three years of death, the lower to gifts during a lifetime.

As a result of the Finance Act, 1975, virtually no DISCRETIONARY TRUSTS were set up between 1974 and 1982. But with the Finance Act of that year, which introduced exemptions – particularly that of gifts between spouses – and reduced rates, the effect of the tax tapered off sharply from its dramatic start. The result of spouse exemption had just begun to unwind and the yield from CTT to rise in real terms when the 1986 Finance Act replaced it with INHERITANCE TAX.

Car. For the purposes of assessment, a car is defined as any mechanically propelled road vehicle except:

(a) a vehicle of a construction primarily suited for the conveyance of goods;
(b) a vehicle of a type not commonly used as a private vehicle, and unsuitable for that use;
(c) a motor cycle or an invalid carriage.

Incidentally it was held that a hearse was not a motor vehicle as it was not for the carriage of persons, a corpse not being such for VAT).

As far as employees are concerned, a car falls into two categories.

(a) It can be owned and used by an employee for the purpose of his employment.

In such circumstances he would be entitled to claim capital allowances at 25 per cent on the written down value basis, less any adjustment for private use – that is, in the first year he would be given 25 per cent of the cost of the car, in the second year 25 per cent of the cost less the allowance already given and so on. If the car cost over £8,000 the allowance is restricted to £2,000 until the balance brought forward falls below £8,000. Any contribution by the employer to the employee's motoring expenses, including CAPITAL ALLOWANCES, reduces the amount claimable against tax.

(b) It can be owned by the employer and used by the employee.

This complicates the issue which was first legislated for in its present form in 1976 and, as far as petrol was concerned, in 1981. The legislation only refers to directors and higher paid employees. The BENEFIT arising is decided by the age, cost and cylinder capacity of the car according to a table laid down for each tax year and there are separate rules for the provision of a car and for the provision of petrol by the employer (see below). An employee whose car falls into the category INSUBSTANTIAL BUSINESS USE (that is, under 2,500 miles annually) is taxed on 1.5 times the car scale rate, but not the petrol scale rate; if, however, business use is over 18,000 miles annually the car scale rate only is halved. The car scale rate is deemed to cover all expenses directly incurred by the employer apart from the cost of providing a chauffeur, which must always be treated as additional cost. Any contribution to the employer's cost by the employee reduces the car scale benefit accordingly, but generally not the petrol scale benefit. No benefit at all arises if the employee uses a 'pool' car, which is defined as a car used by two or more employees where any non-business use of the car is incidental and it is not kept overnight on or near an employee's residence (see POOLED CAR).

The position on petrol was unsatisfactory because if the employee was reimbursed, he suffered a taxable benefit; if the employer paid the garage direct he did not. From April 6, 1983, therefore, where fuel is provided for a car made available to a director or higher paid employee, he is treated as having received an emolument equal to the cash equivalent of that benefit fixed by reference to a table of scale benefits similar to that in operation for cars. This benefit can be cancelled if in fact the employee pays for private petrol.

Caravans. Relief on loan interest is available when the loan is for buying a caravan or motor caravan for use as the owner's principal private residence – but not for a tent.

Cases of Schedule E. See SCHEDULE E. See also RESIDENCE ABROAD.

Case stated. A statement drafted by the GENERAL or SPECIAL COMMISSION-ERS after an appeal hearing where dissatisfaction has been expressed. It states the facts of the case, the contentions of the parties and the determination (decision) of the Commissioners for the ruling of the High Court; see OBJECTIONS AND APPEALS and DISSATISFACTION, EX-PRESSION OF.

Cash voucher. Any voucher, stamp or similar document capable of being exchanged for a sum greater than, equal to or not substantially less than the expense incurred by the employer providing it, unless the sum, if paid directly to the recipient, would not have been chargeable to income tax under Schedule E, for example, under a suggestion scheme.

Casual earnings. If casual earnings cannot be dealt with under the PAYE system, they may be assessed directly and the recipient in effect operates his own deduction scheme, known as the DP (direct payment) procedure. Careful records should be kept of such earnings and expenses, if any.

Centre I. The name of the first computer centre for PAYE. In East Kilbride, it covers the whole of Scotland's Schedule E assessments. It was set up as far back as 1968. The Revenue expects nationwide computerisation of PAYE by 1995 under their COP (computerisation of PAYE) plans.

Certificate of pay, tax deducted and NIC. A form in triplicate which the employer completes at the end of the tax year. It is headed 'End of Year Return P14' and, with the usual particulars of name and address, gives full details of the tax position of the employee over the year. The top two copies go to the Inspector, who forwards one to the DHSS; the bottom copy, numbered P60, is handed to the taxpayer.

Certificate of Full Disclosure. A certificate, the wording of which is usually suggested by the Revenue, which a taxpayer is asked to complete at the end of an investigation case where irregularities have been disclosed (see INVESTIGATION). It certifies the complete disclosure of all income, assets and facts bearing on the taxpayer's tax affairs. Its completion and signature is a serious matter; its contents must be carefully checked.

Chancellor of the Exchequer. In simple terms, the keeper of the national purse, responsible for the country's revenue both from borrowing and taxation. He probably ranks third in the cabinet pecking order after the prime minister and the foreign secretary. In the early part of the 19th century the office was not as prestigious as it later became: WILLIAM PITT THE YOUNGER and SIR ROBERT PEEL as prime ministers introduced the budgets imposing and reimposing income tax. It was some of the later Victorian chancellors, notably W E Gladstone, who enhanced the status of the office, which has remained high to this day.

Chargeable gain. A gain assessable to CAPITAL GAINS TAX arising on the DISPOSAL of a chargeable asset (this excludes *inter alia* cars and national savings certificates). It may be subject to time apportionment where the asset was owned on April 5, 1965. Certain gains are not chargeable: of these the most important is that arising on an individual's PRINCIPAL PRIVATE RESIDENCE. Others are small gifts, currency acquired for personal use outside the UK, awards for valour, gambling winnings, compensation, life assurance policies and deferred annuities, chattels, works of art and so on given for the public benefit and the transfer on retirement of a business or shares in a family trading company when retirement relief is available (see RETIREMENT).

Charges on income. Deductible in arriving at TOTAL INCOME and comprise annual payments made by the taxpayer under a legal obligation from which he is entitled to deduct tax; such a taxpayer must in due course prove he has paid tax at least at basic rate on an equivalent amount of income. An example of such a payment is a DEED OF COVENANT. Interest payable also ranks as a deduction in so far as it is allowable for tax purposes and has not otherwise been allowed; also 50 per cent of Class IV national insurance contributions payable for the year of assessment.

Charities. Charities are generally exempt from income tax and CAPITAL GAINS TAX in respect of income and gains directly applied to charitable purposes.
   The standard way of making charitable payments is by DEED OF COVENANT, which gives the charity the amount covenanted plus the tax on it, while the covenantor only pays over the net amount (see CHARGES). As far as simple subscriptions to charities are concerned, it is unlikely they could be claimed as Schedule E expenses. Following the 1986 Finance Act, however, there is a new scheme operating from April 1987 enabling employers, acting through approved charity agents, to operate 'net pay' arrangements (see SUPERANNUATION) on donations by employees up to £100 a year.

Child. In general, 'child' refers to a relationship not to age: legally a child is a person under 14 years of age (Children and Young Persons Act, 1933). In relation to ADDITIONAL PERSONAL ALLOWANCE, the definition includes a stepchild of the claimant, a child born originally out of wedlock if the parents marry subsequently, and an adopted child if that child was under 18 years when adopted.

Child benefit. A tax-free indexed allowance payable usually to the mother either in cash or direct to a bank account. Child benefit took the place of child allowance which, with minor exceptions, was abolished in 1979/80.

Clergymen and ministers of religion. Their emoluments are assessable under Schedule E and tax is deducted under PAYE. There is no assessment on any benefit from a clergyman's residence and gardens, but if he pays rent he is allowed up to 25 per cent of that, together with any repairs. He is also entitled to claim expenses such as postage, paper, telephone, car expenses incurred in his parochial duties, and any fees paid to a locum by concession. Gifts, such as EASTER OFFER-INGS, are assessable but not where paid in recognition of past services.

Religious communities are in a special category; if they are not treated as charities, a proportion of the aggregate income of the Order is allocated to each member tax free; it is less than single allowance. But if earnings are received – say as a teacher – and handed over to the Order, the recipient is still assessable under Schedule E.

Ministers of other Christian denominations are basically dealt with in the same way as ministers of the Church of England and will be allowed the same type of expenses. Ministers, priests and teachers of other religions may not fall within the ambit of Schedule E but may well be more correctly assessable under Schedule D as exercising a vocation. They will also be able to claim expenses wholly and exclusively incurred in the performance of their duties.

Close company. Can be defined briefly as a family company but technically it is one controlled by five or fewer participators (individuals with claims on the company such as shares, loans or voting rights) or of participators who are directors. Previously such companies could be penalised in tax terms where they retained their profits instead of distributing them to shareholders as DIVIDENDS, but these constraints have been largely removed as regards trading companies.

Clothing. Expenditure on protective clothing is allowable, and uniforms and so on provided by the employer are not assessable as a benefit because they are not convertible into cash although the Revenue may challenge this. An employer's gift of clothing is assessable on the second-hand value of the garments so provided except for higher paid employees. Expenditure on ordinary clothing is not normally allowable, even when it is bought for a specific purpose – such as appearance professionally in court – since it also fulfils the normal requirement of having to be dressed.

Club membership fees. If they are paid by the employer they are assessable; if they are paid by the employee they are not allowed as a deduction even where required by the job. They can, however, be allowed when they entitle the member to cheaper accommodation.

Coding. See NOTICE OF CODING.

Collector of taxes. Originally appointed by the General Commissioners and not until 1945 did all Collectors become appointees of the Board of Inland Revenue, under whose direction they now act. Their main duties are to collect due and payable tax and to levy DISTRAINT when tax is not paid. Collection has become increasingly centralised: there are two main Accounts Offices at Cumbernauld and Shipley. It should be noted that the Collector acts under the instructions of the INSPECTOR OF TAXES and disputes over the amount of tax payable on any amount normally have to be dealt with by the Inspector. Arrangements for delayed payment or instalments of an agreed amount are, however, made with the Collector.

Commercial traveller. Today the description representative or salesman is more often used. As far as his expenses are concerned, the cost of travelling in the course of business activities is allowable; some expenses for using part of the home as an office may also be allowable if a good deal of paperwork needs to be done there and perhaps also an amount for his wife's wages. A good case will have to be made and, of course, careful records are essential.

Commission. When remuneration is paid in the form of salary and commission, tax is deducted from both sources under PAYE. Note also that businesses which habitually pay commissions either to their own employees or others are required to make an annual return of these payments; there is a penalty for failure to comply. The payment of compensation for breaking an agreement to pay commission is normally assessable if the commission itself would have been.

Compensation for loss of office. The first step in considering the assessability of a sum receivable by an employee on the termination of his employment is to decide whether it is taxable according to the general rules of Schedule E. For instance, the following are not generally regarded as assessable.

(a) Death benefits and sums in respect of injury.
(b) Voluntary payments held to be personal testimonials.
(c) Lump sums to the extent that the individual's duties included periods of foreign service.
(d) Payments in commutation of an agreed pension.

Where a charge arises, as with normal compensation, current legislation exempts the first £25,000 of such a payment (GOLDEN HANDSHAKE). The excess over this sum is progressively reduced as follows.

Next £25,000, tax reduced by one half (but see below).
Next following £25,000, tax reduced by one quarter.
Excess over £75,000, no reduction.

As usual there are payments which do not fall within the non-taxable or taxable category.

(a) *Restrictive covenants.* Here the tax liability is computed by GROSSING UP the amount paid at basic rate, then charging higher rate tax on the gross amount less the notional basic rate included in the grossing up.
(b) *Variation of service agreements.* It depends on the facts of the case whether a particular payment can be argued as being for past or future services or exempt. If the duties remain more or less the same, the amount would seem to be assessable; if there was a radical change and a possible claim for compensation the amount would seem to be capital. But generalisations are dangerous.
(c) *Inducing an individual to take up new employment.* The usual attitude of the Revenue is to regard any sums paid in this context as advance remuneration. See GOLDEN HANDCUFFS and GOLDEN HELLO.

It cannot be too strongly emphasised that, in relation to termination payments generally, a payment labelled, say, as recognising past services will be taxed in full as additional remuneration for these services. Great care should be taken with documentation, minutes and correspondence so that the Revenue cannot argue that such termination payments are taxable. The formalities with regard to *ex gratia* payments should never be undertaken until after the employee concerned has stopped work. Professional advice should always be sought before any decisive step is taken, not after, when it may be too late.

In June 1986 the Revenue admitted that the 1982 legislation was defective in that the next £50,000 was taxable at half normal rates and that full taxation applied only to the excess over £100,000. The legislation has now been corrected but only in respect of termination payments arising on or after June 4, 1986. It is possible, therefore, that individuals who received termination payments in excess of £50,000 before that date have paid too much tax and they should take the matter up with their local INSPECTOR OF TAXES.

Complaints, system for. The statutory system for complaints is, in the first instance, the appeal system (see OBJECTIONS AND APPEALS). If there is some technical reason why that remedy cannot be sought there are available the three PREROGATIVE ORDERS. If there seems to be a question of maladministration, recourse may be had to the OMBUDSMAN.

But most complaints simply concern the way a case has been dealt with (or perhaps not dealt with) in a DISTRICT. In these circumstances, a letter to the District Inspector, marked for his personal attention is the first move. If that gets no response, the matter should be referred to the local REGIONAL CONTROLLER. In the unlikely event of no reply or an unsatisfactory reply, the final approach must be to the BOARD OF INLAND REVENUE itself.

Composite rate. The average rate of income tax which would be payable by bank and building society investors so that the income tax paid by the banks and the societies will approximate that which would have been paid by the individuals had they been directly assessed on an individual basis.

Concessions. See EXTRA-STATUTORY CONCESSIONS.

Connected with the company. Relief for investment in a BUSINESS EXPANSION SCHEME is not available to an individual who is connected with the company. He falls within this definition where he or an associate is:

(a) an employee of the company or of a partner of the company;
(b) a partner of the company;
(c) a director of the company or of another company which is a partner of that company.

An individual is not connected with a company by reason of the above unless he received remuneration as an employee or director during the five years previous to the issue of the shares. The reimbursement of expenses does not prejudice this position.

An individual is connected if he possesses a 30 per cent holding or would be entitled on a winding-up to receive more than 30 per cent of the assets, or controls the company. Where an individual subscribes for shares in a company with which he is not connected, he shall be treated as connected if he has subscribed for the shares as part of an arrangement which provides for another person to subscribe for shares in a company with which he, or any other individual who is party to the arrangement, is connected.

Construction industry employees. A contractor in the construction industry is obliged to deduct tax from payments to subcontractors unless they possess a subcontractor's tax certificate, often referred to as an exemption certificate. The grant of this certificate depends on the subcontractor having an excellent tax record, including the current operation of the PAYE system. Employers in the construction industry, particularly subcontractors, were at one time notorious for a cavalier attitude to PAYE procedures and National Insurance obligations. The position is now much improved. See also GANG LEADER.

Continental Shelf. The Continental Shelf involves an extension of UK tax law to the exploitation of the sea bed covered by UK territorial waters. Foreign employers not resident in the UK are nevertheless required to operate PAYE from emoluments paid to employees working in the Continental Shelf because they are regarded as trading through a branch or agency in the UK.

Conventional or cash basis. If an employee also exercises a trade or profession outside his normal employment, he will need to prepare accounts and the Revenue may not object to their preparation on the *basis of cash* actually received during the period, less expenses actually paid.
Another basis that may be allowed is the *bills rendered basis*, whereby the debtors and creditors of a business are taken into account but not its work in progress – that is, the value of its unbilled work. The Revenue is generally reluctant to allow any business to adopt a conventional or cash basis and in no circumstances will allow it in the first three years of trading. (See, in contrast, EARNINGS BASIS.)

Copyright. Where copyright royalties and public lending rights payments are paid to non-residents, they should be taxed by deduction at source; the payer is assessable even if he has not deducted the tax. Tax would, however, not be deducted where the taxpayer is resident and exercising a vocation assessable under Schedule D, Case II.

Covenant, Deed of. Technically defined as a deed containing an agreement which creates an obligation. There must be evidence of payment and deduction of tax, it must not be reciprocal and the attestation clause of the deed requires the word 'sealed'. A covenant to charity must be capable of exceeding three years but for other purposes the required period is six years. A common use is for parents to covenant for their adult student children and the Revenue has devised a model form for this purpose. The tax deducted from the payment made by the parent can be reclaimed by the adult student provided his total income does not bring him over the taxable threshold.

Credit card. Credit cards provided by employers for the payment of employees' bills have been treated as a benefit since 1982. Discount cards, however, issued to employees to enable them to buy goods from their employer at less than retail price were specifically excluded from the legislation and are not taxable.

Cricketer, professional. Like a FOOTBALLER, he is assessable on any remuneration, talent money, bonuses, fees, promotional and advertising payments and personal appearances. The main difference is that his BENEFIT receipts are not assessable. He can claim a deduction for the cost of clothing he uses in his sporting activities.

Current year basis. This is the BASIS OF ASSESSMENT whereby, as in Schedule E, income is charged to tax on the basis of the amount arising in the year of assessment.

D

Day of absence. Defined as a day on which a person is absent at the end of that day. It is relevant when earnings from work done abroad are being considered, because the number of days of absence may determine the amount of relief from UK tax.

Daughter's services. See ALLOWANCES.

Death. Personal representatives of a deceased person are assessable:

(a) for all tax due from the deceased to the date of his death;
(b) to income tax at the basic rate for all income not already taxed received after the death and to capital gains subject to the annual exemption.

The income of an estate consists of aggregate income less INTEREST and CHARGES, sums payable out of residue under the law of intestacy when there is no will and the admissible expenses of administering the estate.

Assessments on deceased persons' income or capital gains accruing before death must be made within three years after the year of assessment in which death took place. Assessments for any of the tax years preceding death may be made within the same time limit if they are for the purpose of making good tax lost to the Revenue by reason of the deceased's NEGLECT, WILFUL DEFAULT or FRAUD. Proceedings for fines or penalties must be started within six years of the date when the offence was committed, but they may be begun against a deceased person's personal representatives at any time.

Deduction of tax. The principle of deduction of tax at source first appeared in British fiscal history during the 17th century and was reintroduced by Addington when in 1803 he revived WILLIAM PITT THE YOUNGER's income tax, which had been repealed during the brief period of peace following the Treaty of Amiens. It was so successful that, with the rate of tax at half the level of Pitt's, the yield was nearly three times greater (£16 million as against £6 million) when Waterloo marked the end of the Napoleonic War in 1815.

That success has continued to the present day. Income tax may legally be deducted by the payer from annuities, other annual payments and certain royalties. But tax must still be deducted and accounted for to the Revenue when such payments are not paid or not wholly paid out of income brought into charge to tax. Maintenance and separation allowances are subject to deduction of tax and so are interest, dividends and local authority and government stock. Dividends and interest paid by coupons or otherwise are taxed at source. BUILDING SOCIETIES and BANKS are in a special category in that notional tax has been deducted before being paid to the account holders (see COMPOSITE RATE TAX). Mortgage interest on home loans may now be paid after deduction of tax at the basic rate (MIRAS). Finally, perhaps the greatest success of all, PAYE is basically a gigantic tax deduction scheme. Note that in many cases the payee must provide a certificate to show that tax has been deducted in order to be able to reclaim it.

Deductions working sheet. The official title of this is the form P11 (New). It must be kept by the employer for each employee and gives in tabular form, weekly details of pay, tax deducted and related NI contributions. An employer may use his own forms if approved by the Revenue.

Deed of Covenant. See COVENANT, DEED OF.

Deed of Family Arrangement. See FAMILY ARRANGEMENT, DEED OF.

Delayed remittance. This relates to Schedule E, Case III and is a remittance of income which could not be made to the UK for some reason outside the taxpayer's responsibility, for example, if there was currency control where the income arose or foreign currency was not available.

Dentists. The emoluments of dentists holding full-time appointments under the NHS are assessable under Schedule E; part-time appointments are similarly assessable under Schedule E. Appointments outside the NHS are also strictly assessable under Schedule E but if the fees are comparatively small they may be included in the Schedule D receipts, as will fees from other activities outside the scope of official appointments.

Dependent relative, residence provided for. No capital gains liability arises from the sale of a house provided for a dependent relative (see ALLOWANCES) rent free and without any consideration, but in the case of a husband and wife living together only one claim can be allowed during a particular period of assessment. Tax relief is also available for interest on a loan to acquire a property for a dependent relative, subject to the £30,000 limit including any personal loans.

Director. As far as Schedule E benefits legislation is concerned, a director is any person:

(a) in relation to a company whose affairs are managed by a board of directors, a member of that board;
(b) in relation to a company whose affairs are managed by a single director, that director;
(c) in relation to a company whose affairs are managed by the members themselves, a member.

It also includes any person on whose directions the directors of the company are accustomed to act, but not if such a person's advice is professional or consultative only. It also includes any member of a committee which manages an incorporated association.

Directors and higher paid employees. The benefits legislation applies to:

(a) employment as a director of a company, but only if he has a material interest or his employment is as a full-time working director; or
(b) employment with emoluments at the rate of £8,500 currently or more. Note that emoluments include the value of all benefits received as if the employee were higher paid and all expenses reimbursed to the employee before any deduction for allowable expenses: so the amount paid may need quite a lot of adjustment for the purposes of this test.

Dirty money. An additional payment for performing unpleasant or unsocial tasks by, for example, dustmen or sewage workers. It is assessable but special protective clothing may be needed, the cost of which would be allowable.

Disabled persons. Disability is one of the conditions which defines a *dependent relative* (see ALLOWANCES). A disabled person's vehicle maintenance grant is not assessable to tax.

Discovery. The word has been in the Acts for over a century. It refers to the making of further assessments following the discovery of an omission of income and an overallowance of some relief. It has been held to mean 'comes to the conclusion', 'finds or is satisfied', 'has reason to believe', or more recently, 'it newly appears'. It does not, however, cover a case where all the facts were clearly presented but wrongly interpreted; a later, correct, interpretation is not a discovery.

Discretionary trust. As the name implies, a trust in which the trustees have a discretion to apply the income and the capital for the benefit of beneficiaries as they may think fit. Income is taxed at the additional rate of 16 per cent in addition to the basic rate (giving a total, currently, of 45 per cent) unless it is a charity or the income is treated as that of the settlor. Discretionary payments by the trustees are treated as net of tax equivalent to the basic rate plus the additional rate mentioned.

Dispensation. The requirement that every employer must notify the Revenue of all benefits on form P11D may be modified by applying for a dispensation from having to declare routine expenses and benefits payments in return for an assurance that such payments will be covered by an equivalent amount of expense deduction.

One effect of this is payments covered by a dispensation are part of an employee's remuneration for any tax purpose, in particular the £8,500 a year test (see DIRECTORS AND HIGHER PAID EMPLOYEES). Once granted, this dispensation remains in force subject to a testing of whether the original conditions still apply by the Revenue from time to time. Any dispensation granted may be subject to specific conditions imposed by the Revenue; in particular, it will not normally be possible for an individual who would otherwise be a higher paid employee to be taken out of that category because of relief under a dispensation.

Disposal. A term used in connection with Capital Gains Tax and includes a part-disposal. It relates to any CAPITAL RECEIPT derived from disposing of an asset. The actual amount received for the disposal is normally agreed between seller and purchaser at the time of disposal. Capital gains liability on the proceeds may not necessarily arise; they may be among the number of exemptions incorporated in the capital gains tax legislation.

Disposition. A technical word which includes any agreement, arrangement, covenant or trust; in general it means a settlement; and also, in relation to the settlor's own children, any transfer of assets. It is possible to distinguish between arrangements which constitute a settlement and commercial transactions without any element of bounty.

Dissatisfaction, expression of. After the COMMISSIONERS have given their decision at an appeal meeting (see OBJECTIONS AND APPEALS) it is open to either the Inspector or the appellant to express dissatisfaction with the outcome. Action should be taken 'immediately' (though this has been interpreted to mean 'within reasonable time'). The expression is a preliminary to asking the Commissioners to state a case for a hearing in the High Court; a fee of £25, currently, is required for this. The request for a stated case, however, does not commit the party which requested it to proceed to the High Court (see CASE STATED).

Distraint. The seizure of goods and chattels – for example, furniture or a television set – of a person who neglects or refuses to pay tax charged upon demand to the Collector. He will have confirmed with the Inspector before taking this action that the tax is legally collectible.

Districts. Tax districts were once based on the old land tax parishes and in country towns, this may still be so. In general, however, administrative convenience is the main criterion, not geography. They are still situated in all large towns and rural areas and are controlled by the District Inspector. At one time districts dealt with the liabilities of all taxpayers in the locality. Lately, however, London districts in particular have lost their Schedule E cases to special Schedule E districts outside London so that there are now three types of district: the old conventional district which deals with all liabilities in the locality; the districts which deal with all liabilities apart from Schedule E; and the Schedule E districts which have taken over these liabilities. Recently districts in the larger towns have amalgamated so the total number of districts in the country has fallen. See LONDON PROVINCIAL DISTRICTS.

Divers and diving supervisors. They are subject to special rules provided they are employed as divers in operations to exploit the seabed or as a supervisor of such operations. The effect of the rules is that such duties are regarded as assessable under Schedule D, Case I and not Schedule E as would normally be the case.

Dividends. Payments made out of a company's profits to its share-holders. From 1973/74, a UK resident receives in addition to the cash amount of the dividend a tax credit showing the advance corporation tax paid on it by the company. This is equivalent to basic rate tax on the total of dividend plus tax credit. The total of the tax credit plus the dividend is assessable on the shareholder but his tax liability is reduced by the tax credit which effectively cancels out his tax liability if he is only liable at the basic rate. (See TAX CREDIT.)

Divorce. A warning: volumes could (and have) been written on the tax consequences of divorce. The general effects are as follows.

(a) The husband is entitled to the full personal allowance for the year in which the couple became permanently separated.
(b) The wife's income is deemed to be that of her husband up to the date of separation, subject to any election for separate taxation.
(c) The wife is entitled to single person's allowance against her income from the date of separation.
(d) Interest payable by each of the spouses on property held on joint tenancy will continue to be allowable and may be increased since the £30,000 limit will apply to each person.

This is a difficult area and professional advice may be needed.

Doctors. Like those of DENTISTS, the emoluments of a doctor employed by the NHS, whether in a full-time or part-time capacity, are assessable under Schedule E, but, as agreed between the Revenue and the British Medical Association, fees for outside lectures and consultations continue to be assessable under Schedule D. In general, appointments outside the NHS, although strictly assessable under Schedule E, can be brought within the Schedule D assessment if they are not large. Regular engagement as a locum for colleagues in private practice attracts a Schedule D assessment, but an engagement as a locum by a hospital board falls within Schedule E.

Domicile. There is no single definition of domicile. The concept is complicated, affecting the whole of an individual's rights and duties. Briefly, it is the country which a person looks on as his natural homeland. 'Domicile of origin' prevails unless a 'domicile of choice' can be proved, the onus of proof resting on the individual to substantiate that he has acquired a domicile of choice. The test is a mixed question of fact and law.

Of the two types of domicile, *domicile of origin* is acquired at birth; for a legitimate child it is the domicile of the father at the time of birth. To acquire a *domicile of choice*, there must exist the presence or residence in the new country, the intention of remaining there for the foreseeable future and evidence that the individual has given up his domicile of origin. Length of stay is not as significant as fixed intention. For instance, if an individual intended to stay in the UK and only to return to his domicile of origin if his health deteriorated, he could be regarded as having acquired a domicile of choice in the UK as his intention of leaving would be too remote.

Until 1974 a married woman assumed a *domicile of dependence* on marriage, that of her husband. Since then her domicile is determined independently of that of her husband in the same way as that of any other person.

Domicile is important for income tax purposes because an individual, who is resident but *not* domiciled in the UK is liable to UK tax on investment income and gains arising overseas only if they are remitted to this country. He may also be entitled to a measure of relief against his earned income. The definition of domicile is specifically modified for IHT/CTT purposes, so that any individual who has been resident in the UK for at least 17 out of the last 20 years is automatically treated – but for those purposes only – as domiciled in the UK. See also RESIDENT and ORDINARILY RESIDENT.

Double taxation relief. A simple conception but often a complicated calculation. Double taxation occurs when income is taxable in two countries – that is, where it arises in one country but the recipient is taxable in another. Relief may be obtained under the specific terms of a double tax agreement – the UK has comprehensive agreements with most developed countries – under special arrangements and under UNILATERAL DOUBLE TAX RELIEF provisions.

E

Earned income. The principal sources of earned income are as follows.

(a) Any office or employment of profit – that is, Schedule E sources – and from property related.

(b) The personal carrying on of a trade, profession or vocation – that is, income assessable under Schedule D.

(c) Deferred pay, pensions, and so on, given in respect of past services including Civil List pensions, voluntary pensions and compensation for loss of office.

(d) Social security benefits other than specified exemptions.

(e) FURNISHED HOLIDAY LETTING where it is specifically treated as equivalent to a trade.

See also EMOLUMENTS.

Earnings basis. The normal method of computing profits for a period by reference to amount receivable and expenses payable. That means income earned but not paid, expenses incurred and stock and work in progress are, therefore, taken into account. For Schedule E purposes, this basis is applied where an employee has fluctuating emoluments. His remuneration paid in respect of his company's accounting period may be allocated in a pro rata basis to the overlapping tax years. For example, if his company's year end is September, half the remuneration charged in the accounts will be allocated to the tax years ending in the previous April, the other half in the tax year ending next April.

Easter offerings. Gifts to a clergyman, voluntary subscriptions, collections and Easter offerings are assessable according to the general principle that payments for special services are taxable under Schedule E if they are received by virtue of the office even though they are given voluntarily. But if these payments are in recognition of past services they may or may not be taxable, depending on the circumstances.

Educational and scholarship schemes. A director or a higher paid employee is liable to tax on the value of a scholarship awarded by reason of his employment to a member of his family or household. This addition to BENEFITS dates from 1983 following a failure in the Courts to tax such a payment. Apart from this, income from a *bona fide* scholarship is not assessable to tax on the recipient.

Emoluments. The word 'emoluments' includes all 'salaries, fees, wages, perquisites and profits whatsoever', in the words of the Act. For most practical purposes it means money, or money's worth, EXPENSES, certain forms of VOUCHERS and some GIFTS received by virtue of an office or employment. Gifts made on personal grounds and not by way of payment for services are, however, excluded.

Employee. Not until 1922 were employments transferred from Schedule D to Schedule E and put alongside 'offices' already in that Schedule. An employee is, therefore, the holder of an office or a post, and is part and parcel of the organisation for which he works, whether he is a director taking part in the management of the organisation or an employee submitting to orders. For an employment to exist, there must be a master and servant relationship, a contract *of* service as distinct from one *for* services.

Employer. From a Schedule E point of view, the employer is responsible for the operation of the PAYE system: from week to week and month to month this means the deduction of tax from EMPLOYEES' wages plus their graduated insurance contributions and the payment of these to the Collector within 14 days after the end of each month. He must on application give particulars of remuneration paid to his employees including expenses and assessable benefits for any period up to six years before the year of assessment for which application is made. PAYE AUDIT teams review whether the PAYE procedures have been properly carried out.

Where errors are discovered, it is the employer who is responsible for making good any shortfall in accounting for PAYE or NATIONAL INSURANCE CONTRIBUTIONS that should have been deducted from employees' pay.

Employment abroad. Tax liability in the UK depends on DOMICILE (a person's natural home), RESIDENCE (where he has physically been during the tax year) and ORDINARY RESIDENCE (where he is habitually resident). The basic rule for British nationals working overseas, if non-resident, is that they are taxed in the UK only in so far as their remuneration is attributable to any duties of the employment which are performed in the UK. Concessionally any INCIDENTAL DUTIES in the UK are ignored.

Certain categories of non-residents can claim a proportion of their personal allowance and DOUBLE TAXATION RELIEF but if a person ordinarily resident in the UK works overseas for more than a year he will not be assessed on the relevant emoluments whether remitted or not; for short absences (up to 364 days) there is now no relief. If a person is not ordinarily resident he will be assessable on the amounts remitted to the UK in respect of overseas duties.

Enquiry Branch. The first Enquiry Branch office was set up by the Board of Inland Revenue in 1920. There are now ten spread round the country, three of them in London. They specialise in investigating cases of serious fraud, substantial problems involving groups of companies and the deficiencies of corrupt or incompetent accountants. Such cases would normally be referred to the nearest Enquiry Branch by the local tax district, if the understatement of profit amounted to at least £50,000. Its officers are full-time specialists on investigation work and anyone involved in a case referred to an Enquiry Branch needs immediate professional advice. Obviously it would be unusual for Enquiry Branch to be called in over a Schedule E liability although it might be involved in a large expenses and benefits case, especially if more than one director was implicated. See also SPECIAL INVESTIGATION SECTION, SPECIAL OFFICE.

Enquiry Offices. As many Schedule E assessments are not made in the local districts but in special Schedule E districts (see DISTRICTS), difficulties may arise if an interview is called for. When that happens, most large towns have enquiry offices to which a taxpayer's file can be sent and where it can be discussed most conveniently. This facility is not confined to Schedule E cases: any taxpayer can have his file sent on request to the nearest enquiry office if an interview is felt to be helpful. There are nearly 100 of these offices, but if necessary the nearest tax office will also help. The telephone directory heading is: 'Inland Revenue – Taxes H. M. Inspector of' (*not* Collector).

Entertainment. See BUSINESS ENTERTAINMENT, STAFF ENTERTAINMENT.

Error or mistake claim. A relief claimable by any person who has been overcharged because of some error or mistake in a return, other than a change in fiscal practice or legislation; any claim for relief must be made within six years of the end of the tax year concerned. Any appeal against a refusal to grant the relief must be made to the SPECIAL COMMISSIONERS.

Evasion. Evasion of tax, which is outside the law, is usually contrasted with AVOIDANCE, which is within the law. It involves either FRAUD in all its various forms or concealment of the full facts with the aim either of escaping tax or obtaining unwarranted relief. Cases involving fraud are almost invariably dealt with by ENQUIRY BRANCH; the PENALTIES imposed may be severe and the taxpayer may be prosecuted.

Examination expenditure. If an employer pays the expenses of courses and examination fees for an employee, they would normally be allowed and not assessable as benefits, because they are not convertible into cash. But if, for example, an articled clerk pays the expenses out of his salary, they are not allowable, because he can perform the duties without incurring education fees. Even if the employer pays educational fees but the employee pays travel and text book costs, those expenses would not be allowable as being in the performance of the duties. The same criteria would apply to a teacher taking courses to improve his expertise. But examination prizes are not assessable. If an employee is under 21 when the course starts, the training can be a course of general education. Otherwise, it must be training to acquire knowledge or skills necessary for, or to enable him to perform more effectively, his job.

Training expenses include course fees, the cost of essential books and, provided he is absent from work for less than twelve months and will return there at the end of the training, travelling expenses and reasonable payments for subsistence.

An employee who bears such expenses himself can be allowed a deduction from taxable emoluments provided he receives a full salary during the course but is allowed time off to attend it during normal working hours.

The course must be one which the employee is required or encouraged to attend by his employer, full-time for at least four weeks in the UK. But courses to enable the employee to re-sit an examination do not qualify.

Ex gratia payments. *Ex gratia* means literally 'out of favour' and if it can be proved that a payment by an employer to an employee had no connection with the employment, then it would not be assessable. But proving this essential condition may be difficult; and if the motive for making the payment was non-business, the further question arises of the donor's claim for it to be allowed as a deduction.

Expenses. The expenses rule for Schedule E is notoriously restrictive. To take the words of the Act, the following phrases need particular attention:

(a) necessarily obliged to incur and defray;
(b) wholly, exclusively and necessarily; and
(c) in the performance of the said duties.

All these phrases have been the subject of frequent judicial comment. Nevertheless the scope of the rule has hardly widened. To summarise briefly: the expenditure must be incurred and paid for; it must necessarily be incurred, apart from the two preceding adverbs, virtually as a condition of employment; and it must be in the performance not simply because of. Certainly the question of allowability is primarily one of fact: but the principles by which those facts have to be judged are so tightly drawn that time and again taxpayers have found themselves with little room for manoeuvre, although the Revenue may by concession allow part expenditure even when the whole does not qualify.

With regard to expenses incurred by the employee wholly, exclusively and necessarily in the performance of his duties and reimbursed by his employer, these are allowable. It is only when round sum allowances are paid, or possibly expenses are paid in advance, that problems can arise. See DISPENSATIONS and FLAT RATE EXPENSES. See also TRAVELLING EXPENSES, WHOLLY, EXCLUSIVELY AND NECESSARILY.

Explanatory pamphlets. See BOARD'S PAMPHLETS.

Extra-statutory concessions. Because statutorily the BOARD OF INLAND REVENUE is entrusted with the care and management of the direct taxes, they have also the power to grant extra-statutory concessions, which by now have grown into a considerable body of quasi-legislation. The Board publicises any new concessions by means of press releases and complete lists of them are to be found in tax text books and special publications relating solely to them, obtainable from legal booksellers.

F

Family allowances. Payments under the social security system were replaced in 1977 by CHILD BENEFIT which is free of tax. Family income supplement, available to families on low incomes, is also free of tax.

Family arrangement, deed of. This is relevant in the context of IHT, CTT and CGT, and consists of a deed whereby dispositions under a will (or intestacy) are either varied by the beneficiaries concerned or other members of the family are joined as beneficiaries. A less formal arrangement may also be made. Provided the variation is made within two years of death it is related back to the death and not treated as a further disposal or transfer of value.

Fees. See EMOLUMENTS.

Feme sole. A term usually applied to a married woman who is independent of her husband as regards property, but it can also refer to a single woman or a widow.

Finance Act. The Finance Act is the eventual enactment of the Finance Bill, which is presented to the House of Commons by the chancellor in his budget speech, usually on a Tuesday in March or April each year. There follows a general debate on the budget resolution. The Bill is then read for the first time and published within three weeks. After the second reading certain clauses are dealt with by a committee of the whole House, the balance going to a standing committee of about 35 members. Then follows what some experts consider to be too short a process of consideration, often involving the notorious all-night sittings, 'nocturnalisation' as one chancellor termed it. The Bill is then reprinted for the Report Stage and consideration of new clauses before the third reading. The Lords may debate the Bill but have no power of amendment; their second and third readings are usually on the same day and the royal assent follows immediately. Because income tax is an annual tax there is a Provisional Collection of Taxes Act, which in effect keeps all previous enactments in force until the passing of the annual Finance Act. This has to be done by August 4 each year.

Fiscal drag. Not, as might be thought, the CHANCELLOR OF THE EXCHEQUER garbed as Dame Edna Everage, but a technical phrase to indicate a condition where an increase in earnings brings a higher rate of tax into operation, although in real terms, taking inflation into account, there has been no real increase. It can also be used to describe the difference between the actual yield of tax and the potential yield if tax receipts had increased in line with earnings.

Fixed trust. In a fixed trust, the trust deed sets out the share or interest which each beneficiary is entitled to take. This means that each beneficiary is the effective owner of the specified interest which he has been given. The trustee may deduct tax before payment or notify particulars of the beneficiaries to the Revenue for assessment on them personally.

Flat rate expenses. These must be distinguished from round sum allowances. They are the deductions agreed, very often with the trade unions concerned, for tools, special and protective clothing and so on, mainly for manual workers. The Revenue publishes lists of the amounts agreed from time to time. The amounts vary from £25 to £80 but if further expenditure can be justified it should be claimed. The initial cost of such items is not allowable and the clothing must not be adaptable for ordinary wear.

Footballer, professional. He is assessable on any remuneration, fees, promotional and advertising payments arising from his contract with his club in the year; receipts from a BENEFIT or transfer fees can be spread. Payments for travel to a home ground may be allowable for a short time after a transfer. See also CRICKETER.

Forces, armed. The general PAYE regulations apply to the armed forces in the same way as they do to civilians but there are certain modifications: for instance, an appeal against coding may be made to the SPECIAL COMMISSIONERS. Then again there are a number of exemptions. Mess, ration allowances and certain bounties and gratuities are free of tax, but there is no allowance for lodging expenses or for mess expenses. Territorial Army pay is assessable but not the training expenses – or the annual bounty. Other exempt items are travel facilities and terminal grants.

Foreign dividends. Defined as any INTEREST, DIVIDENDS or other ANNUAL PAYMENT payable out of the stock funds, shares or securities of any body of persons not resident in the UK. They are normally assessable on a PREVIOUS YEAR BASIS on the full amount arising, but DOUBLE TAXATION or UNILATERAL RELIEF may be allowable against the tax chargeable. If the payment is by coupon, UK income tax will normally have been deducted. Sometimes double taxation relief will have been allowed and a rate of tax deducted lower than the basic rate. This fact should be noted when the income is set out on a return.

Foreign emoluments. These are paid to any person not domiciled (see DOMICILE) in the UK by an employer who is not RESIDENT in the UK.

They are assessed under SCHEDULE E, Case III, when the duties are performed wholly abroad, but the other two cases of Schedule E may have to be considered when the duties are carried on partly or wholly in the UK. The percentage deductions available for these emoluments before 1983/84 are now being phased out. Deductions may be allowed for necessary expenses; and travelling expenses provided by the employer to the employee and his family for the journey to take up appointment and to return home and for up to two return journeys a year are not assessable.

Fraud. The Courts have never ventured to lay down a precise definition of fraud. It is generally considered to be proved when it is shown that a false representation has been made knowingly, without belief in its truth or recklessly, without caring whether it is true or false. Such cases are normally dealt with by ENQUIRY BRANCH. The Revenue very rarely uses the word in correspondence, although the bulk of BACK DUTY cases are fraudulent on a strict definition, preferring the expression 'wilful default'. See EVASION.

Franklin, Benjamin. The American author, natural philosopher and statesman, who originated the celebrated aphorism: 'There are two certain things in this world, death and taxes.' It was an anonymous 20th century wit who added: 'And death, thank God, doesn't get any worse.'

Free of tax. Like other fiscal phrases this does not always mean what it seems to imply. Basically it denotes the payment of a sum which, after deduction of tax, produces the stipulated amount; it does not mean a payment clear of all deductions. The precise meaning of the words should always be made clear if a payment is so described. For instance, BUILDING SOCIETY INTEREST is said loosely to be free of tax; but it is not free of higher rate tax and the gross amount must be considered when dealing with, say, AGE ALLOWANCE.

Furnished holiday letting. The 1984 Finance Act produced a new area for tax efficient investment, the holiday home. There must be commercial letting – that is, with a view to the realisation of profits – and holiday accommodation is defined as accommodation which must be available for commercial letting to the public generally for at least 140 days in a twelve month period and is so let for at least 70 such days. Subject to these and other conditions relating to the length of time it is occupied by the same tenant(s), the letting is treated as a trade with appropriate deductions from the receipts. It is, therefore, a useful source of income for a married woman, who is not otherwise gainfully occupied, since it is EARNED INCOME and WIFE'S EARNED INCOME RELIEF is available against the profits. The letting of caravans is included.

Furnished letting. Income from casual furnished letting is normally assessable under SCHEDULE D, Case VI although, depending upon how much the landlord is involved and how often the accommodation is let, it may amount to a trade. This is a question of fact and there is some reluctance on the part of the Revenue to admit SCHEDULE D, Case I. Similar considerations also apply to the letting of caravans. The profits are the gross receipts less allowable expenses including a deduction for depreciation of furniture and fittings at 10 per cent (or the renewals basis) – that is, the cost of replacing an identical article.

G

'Gang leader'. The term 'contractor' in the context of the construction industry includes also a gang leader whose gang members work for him and are regarded as self-employed. He will then be rated as a sub-contractor and will receive payment for the work done by the gang. In these circumstances the gang leader is either the employer of the gang members, in which case he must operate PAYE, or must be regarded as a contractor, in which case the members of his gang are sub-contractors who come within PAYE. Briefly, it is unsafe not to deduct tax if in doubt; far better to consult the local INSPECTOR OF TAXES.

General commissioners. Once responsible for the assessment and collection of income tax. Now only their appeal function remains, apart from extended time assessments. They are not required to have any special qualifications but are usually local businessmen or women appointed by the Lord Chancellor. Their duty is to hear and determine appeals against assessments or other executive acts of the Revenue such as a refusal to grant allowances or reliefs. They generally sit locally in groups of two or more and are assisted by a clerk, usually a local solicitor. Their proceedings are not open to the public, to preserve confidentiality and are extremely informal. Any taxpayer aggrieved by any action of the Revenue should not hesitate to approach them as they are independent and impartial. Their full title is Commissioners for the General Purposes of the Income Tax Acts. See also SPECIAL COMMISSIONERS.

Ghosts. The investigators of SPECIAL OFFICE give a good deal of time to identifying individuals for whom there is no tax file because they have never admitted to being resident in the UK. Such people are called 'ghosts', for obvious reasons.

Gifts. The assessability of a so-called gift depends whether it arises out of an employment, in which case it is taxable, or whether it has been given to the recipient in a personal capacity, in which case it is not. The difficulty with this distinction is that it is rarely clear-cut. The fact that payments may be voluntary and at random intervals does not make them any the less assessable. See CLERGYMEN, CRICKETER, FOOTBALLER.

Golden handcuffs. Often when a remuneration package is arranged, it includes some form of inducement to stay with the employer. It would be difficult to argue that such an inducement was solely for an undertaking not to leave the employer at an early date and not simply for services paid in advance and therefore assessable.

Golden handshake. See COMPENSATION FOR LOSS OF OFFICE.

Golden hello. The Revenue's view is that an upfront payment is a reward for future services and should be treated as an ordinary salary instalment – this may mean tax at the highest rates if some of the 'signing-on' figures for footballers are correct. An exception to this rule seems to be for rugby players who relinquish their amateur for professional status.

Golden parachute. An amendment to service contracts to provide for a considerable payment if the company is taken over and the executive is dismissed. If, however, the takeover and dismissal occur and payment is made under the terms of the service contract, it will be assessable; if there is damage or compensation, it may escape.

Government securities. (a) Paying agents entrusted in this country with paying interest, public annuities, dividends or shares of annuities out of the public revenue of any public authority or institution outside the UK must deduct tax from such payments at basic rate. See SCHEDULE C.
(b) British government securities are exempt from capital gains; the interest on many holdings is free of tax if beneficially owned by persons not resident in the UK. Most interest is now paid after deduction of tax, but there are exceptions such as the $3\frac{1}{2}$ per cent war loan. Discount on Treasury securities is not assessable on individuals, nor are prizes on premium bonds or interest on national saving certificates except where held in excess of the amount authorised. See INTEREST RECEIVED.

Gratuities. These cannot escape taxation as they are clearly for services rendered. What makes a tip assessable is not only the element of service it represents, but also the expectation of its being received. The Revenue may accept a basic figure to save tedious record-keeping, though it may review this later. When tips are pooled under a TRONC arrangement, the tronc master is responsible for operating PAYE in payments he makes to individuals.

Grossing up. This means arriving at a sum which, when basic rate tax is deducted, comes to the net figure. For instance, building society interest is treated as if exempt from basic rate tax but it has to be grossed up to arrive at the amount liable to higher rates. If basic rate was 20 per cent and net building society interest received was £100, the gross amount would be £125. (Proof: £125 @ 20 per cent = 25 = net £100).

Guide dog. It is possible to make a claim for the upkeep and so on (vets' fees and cost of kennels) of a guide dog which is required in the course of the employment – for example, when a blind teacher needs the dog's help to move from place to place. The Revenue does not press the point of private use if the dog is maintained at the blind person's own expense. The cost of replacing the dog is also allowable.

H

Hansard extract. This is a parliamentary question and answer dated October 5, 1944, which sets out the Board of Inland Revenue's policy for settling investigation cases. It is given to the taxpayer to read before the opening interview in such a case.

It says in effect that the Revenue may take into account the extent to which a taxpayer has cooperated in an investigation in arriving at the level of penalties, but that they will not be bound in advance to allow any mitigation of penalties, nor will they give an undertaking in advance not to prosecute where this may be appropriate.

Hardship. Refers here to financial hardship and is one of the principal factors which the Collector of Taxes would take into account when tax has not been paid and he is considering DISTRAINT. It is also a factor when considering the settlement in an investigation case although the Revenue tends to take a more severe line here as the additional tax payable is due to the taxpayer's neglect, wilful default or fraud.

Headteacher's expenses. It has been held that the cost of attending lectures to widen academic knowledge is not an allowable deduction. On the other hand, the cost of entertaining parents or visitors to a school can be allowed concessionally if properly recorded.

Higher paid employee. See DIRECTORS AND HIGHER PAID EMPLOYEES.

Higher rates. Rates of income tax above the basic rate charged on an individual's total income above a certain level. There are currently five rates above the basic rate in bands of varying amounts.

Hobby. Cynics remark that the Revenue tends to class a trading activity as a hobby if it makes a loss and an assessable trade if it makes a profit so that the loss will not be a loss in trade and so relievable against other income. The question of whether an activity shall be classed as a trade or a hobby is largely a question of fact depending on the clear commercial nature of the enterprise. Special rules apply in the case of farming and market gardening, which generally restrict claims for relief where losses have been incurred for more than five previous years.

Holiday. In the context of BENEFITS, directors and higher paid employees are assessable in full on the cost of a holiday unless combined with a business trip. Even then the holiday element in that trip could be taxable depending on its extent. For lower paid workers there is no liability provided the employer pays direct and does not reimburse the employee.

Holdover relief. When an asset is transferred by way of gift, CAPITAL GAINS TAX is normally chargeable to the donor as if the asset had been transferred at its open market value. However, donor and donee may jointly elect to have the chargeable gain held over; this normally results in the donee inheriting the donor's cost so that the full tax becomes payable on his disposal. If the donee becomes non-resident within six years of the gift and still holds the gifted asset, the holdover gain becomes immediately assessable on him.

Holiday pay. Tax is usually deducted from holiday pay but it may be paid in full. The tax owing may be spread over the whole year or adjusted in the coding. If a holiday stamp scheme is operated, tax is taken at the time of payment at the basic rate.

House. The benefit from the use of accommodation is the gross rateable value (see ANNUAL VALUE) which tends to be lower than the open market rental. From April 6, 1984, where the accommodation cost over £75,000, there is a charge on the excess over cost at the 'official rate of interest' (currently 12 per cent); cost includes any improvements since purchase. See ANNUAL VALUE and REPRESENTATIVE ACCOMMODATION.

Houseboat. Regarded as a suitable asset for loan interest relief where it is used as the owner's principal private residence (see also CARAVAN). It is defined as a boat or similar structure designed or adapted for use as a place of permanent habitation.

Housekeeper relief. See ALLOWANCES (b).

Husband and wife.

(a) The higher personal allowance is due to a married man whose wife is living with him or wholly maintained by him by means of a voluntary allowance. The allowance is not due if the husband makes maintenance payments under a court order or some other enforceable agreement since that can be deducted from his income for tax purposes (see MAINTENANCE). 'Living with' implies living together in intention except where one spouse is absent abroad for a whole year; for that year they are treated as if permanently separated unless it is to their advantage to be treated as still living together. Whether the Courts will recognise a foreign marriage cannot be stated with any certainty, but polygamous marriages have been accepted.

The income of a wife living with her husband is deemed to be his unless that income is received as a trustee or a guardian for others and unless one spouse is not resident (see above) or unless separate assessment is claimed (see below). Tax may be collected from a wife on assessments made on her husband (or his executors) if that assessment could have been on the wife under separate assessment procedure; by contrast a widower (or his executors) may disclaim liability on his wife's unpaid tax within two months of the grant of probate or longer if the personal representatives agree to the disclaimer; the tax may then be extracted from the wife's estate. Note that the Revenue will normally write direct to a married woman about her own tax affairs, even if she has not approached the Revenue in the first place.

In the year of marriage, the wife is assessed as a single person on the whole of her income for the year; the income arising from date of marriage to the subsequent April 5 is not deemed that of her husband (exceptionally this does not apply if the marriage took place on April 6; then the incomes of husband and wife are aggregated for that year). As far as the husband is concerned the married allowance is reduced by one twelfth of the difference between married and single allowance for each fiscal month ending before the wedding date. It follows that there is now no advantageous date for the wedding day as there used to be when the wife, if she continued working, was granted the whole of her single allowance to the date of marriage and the whole of her wife's earned income relief thereafter.

Wife's earned income relief is granted on her earned income including social security retirement pension from her own contributions but excluding any social security benefits. It is not granted in the year of marriage (see above) as she then has the single person's allowance in her own right.

If a marriage ends either by death, divorce or separation, the husband retains his higher personal allowance for that year: the wife is entitled to full single personal allowance from then to the following April 5. As far as MAINTENANCE is concerned, tax is normally deductible, except in the case of SMALL MAINTENANCE PAYMENTS. If under a divorce court order there are payments to the wife for the children, that income is the wife's for tax purposes, but the Court can order payments to the children direct, in which case the income is theirs.

(b) There are two types of separate assessment.

(1) *Separate assessment*, for which application must be made within six months before July 6 in any year of assessment. This has the effect of apportioning the total allowances due to both in proportion to the income of each to their total income. The total tax paid is not affected: it simply means that the income of each bears the appropriate amount of tax attributable to each.

(2) *Separate taxation* of wife's earnings, for which application must be

made not later than twelve months after the end of the year of assessment. The effect is that both husband and wife are treated as single persons assessable on their own incomes. Both get single person's allowance but both get the benefit of the gradually increasing higher rate bands. This election remains in force until jointly revoked; to be tax efficient earnings must be substantial, currently about £26,000 with the lower earnings of the two around £7,000.

If a husband is ignorant of a wife's income, say, in bank interest, the Revenue will by concession make a confidential settlement with her but will expect her to ensure that such income is included in her husband's return in succeeding years.

(c) *Age allowance* is an increase in the single and married allowances available where a person or his wife is aged 65 or more in the year of claim; it substitutes for the ordinary allowances but is subject to an income limit. Where the total income exceeds the limit, the allowance is reduced by two thirds of the excess until the allowance reverts to the ordinary allowances.

(d) Lastly, *widow's bereavement allowance* is granted when the husband dies after April 5. The widow continues to be allowed the higher personal allowance for that year and the year after the year of death (unless she remarries before the beginning of that year). It is given in addition to any other available reliefs.

I

Incapacitated person. The definition in the Taxes Management Act, 1970 is any infant, person of unsound mind, lunatic, idiot or insane person; returns, if they have to be completed, will be made on their behalf by trustees. The word 'incapacitated' may also apply to a dependent relative and is taken to mean that the person is unable to work because of old age or permanent illness or disability.

Incidental duties. These are relevant when the main duties are performed overseas and, if the duties are performed in the UK, they are incidental to those performed abroad (see EMPLOYMENT ABROAD). In the case of non-resident British nationals working abroad such duties are ignored when considering liability to UK tax. It is a question of fact whether they are incidental. As a general rule those duties not involving more than three months outside the normal place of performance of duties are regarded as incidental, but this may depend on the precise significance of those duties. The term is also relevant when considering cases where main duties are exercised in the UK and the incidental duties abroad.

Income. No comprehensive definition of income may be found anywhere in the Taxing Acts. The method of the fiscal legislators has been to classify the various types of income into SCHEDULES and then to devise rules for measuring the income arising from these designated sources. Income is not necessarily cash received but also money's worth as in the case of BENEFITS; it must, however, be received. It must also arise from a recognisable source, a precondition which could arguably take casual receipts out of assessment; and it must partake of the nature of income, not capital: a determining feature here is whether the income arising is annual income.

A feature of sophisticated avoidance schemes has been to contrive the conversion of income into a non-taxable category. This has led to the questioning of income as a tax base in favour of expenditure, but this concept has not so far gained any general acceptance. See also EARNED INCOME and EMOLUMENTS.

Income and Corporation Taxes Act, 1970. The latest consolidation of the income tax Acts: it is known as TA 1970 or ICTA 1970. It is updated annually but there has been so much new legislation that another consolidation is overdue. Tax administration was consolidated in the Taxes Management Act, 1970 (TMA 1970), capital allowances in the Capital Allowances Act, 1968 (CAA 1968) and capital gains tax in the Capital Gains Tax Act, 1979 (CGTA 1979).

In-depth investigation. A procedure which mainly concerns Schedule D taxpayers. Businesses which show low gross profit rates in relation to the same type of business in the same neighbourhood are selected for enquiry into the records and underlying information which the Inspector calls for in order to look into them himself. About 90 per cent of those so examined result in an assessment of additional liability to tax.

Indexation. An allowance for CAPITAL GAINS TAX purposes, introduced in 1982 and substantially modified in 1985 to give some recognition to the effects of inflation. It is found by applying the change in the retail prices index from the date of ACQUISITION or March 1982, whichever is later, to the date of DISPOSAL to whichever is the greater, original cost or market value at March 1982 (if the asset concerned was then owned).

Individuals entering the UK to work. As with EMPLOYMENT ABROAD for UK citizens, the first question for a foreigner coming to this country is to establish his status – that is, to decide on his DOMICILE and whether he is RESIDENT or ORDINARILY RESIDENT here. He will be issued with a questionnaire (form P86) by the Inland Revenue so that this status may be at least provisionally settled. If income is received from a UK resident employer it is charged to UK income tax in full. If income is received from an employer not resident in the UK it is charged to UK income tax when the employee has become resident in this country. There is a foreign earnings deduction, now reduced to 25 per cent, which is to be phased out in 1989/90. Where an individual, not domiciled but resident and ordinarily resident here, performs duties for an employer not resident in the UK wholly outside this country, he will be assessable on the REMITTANCE BASIS. Collection of tax is through PAYE if possible but if not direct collection (see PAYE). Reasonable travelling expenses (see FOREIGN EMOLUMENTS) will not be treated as assessable.

Inheritance tax (IHT). The modified form of CAPITAL TRANSFER TAX, introduced in March 1986. The tax applies to the whole of an individual's estate passing on his death and to certain lifetime gifts. The following lifetime gifts are not subject to tax provided that the donor survives at least seven years from the date of the gift: gifts to individuals; gifts to ACCUMULATION AND MAINTENANCE SETTLEMENTS; gifts to trusts for disabled persons.

There are various exceptions, notably for transfer between husband and wife, and an ANNUAL EXEMPTION of £3,000. There are also reliefs for certain categories of business and agricultural property. There are special rules for gifts where the donor continues to enjoy or is eligible for some benefit.

Inland Revenue press office. An office in SOMERSET HOUSE which acts as the public relations centre. Here are issued press releases and helpful initial information on Revenue affairs generally.

Inspector of Taxes. An Inspector of Taxes is a professional civil servant. He has to pass two departmental examinations before he can be regarded as a full inspector. He acts under the directions of the Board of Inland Revenue and is responsible for the agreement and assessment of all taxpayers' liabilities. He usually represents the Board at appeal meetings (see OBJECTIONS AND APPEALS). He may also have considerable administrative responsibilities when he is in charge of a DISTRICT. Entry to the inspectorate is either by open written examination and interviews or by promotion within the department. The annual intake rarely reaches the number of recruits required and this shortage is exacerbated by resignations for more tempting jobs outside.

Insubstantial business use. The phrase used in the context of benefit from the use of an employer's CAR. The definition is less than 2,500 business miles. An individual whose car falls into this category is taxed on 1.5 times the normal scale rate applicable to the provision of the car (but not to the car petrol scale).

Insurance agents. Their remuneration usually consists of salary and commission both of which are subject to PAYE. As far as expenses are concerned, agents often operate from home so that most of their mileage is in the performance of the duties and so allowable, and would be taken to include visits to the office if only occasional. It is also the practice to allow, for a home-based agent, a proportion of domestic expenses and, if justified, wife's wages.

Interest in possession. A beneficiary has an interest in possession in settled property if he has: a present right of enjoyment of the net income of the settled property without any further decision of the trustees being required.

This stands even where there is a possibility of that right being taken away in the future; but a right to enjoy income subject to a power for the trustees to accumulate precludes an interest in possession.

Interest. For tax purposes, there are three main categories of interest.

(a) *On overdue tax.*
Instituted in 1975 for tax assessable under Schedules A, C, D and E. Interest is chargeable on each assessment, but currently the Board has

power to remit interest of £30 or less; it should be noted that 'on each assessment' includes the aggregate of interest on each instalment in the case of Schedule D.

The rate of interest, currently 9 per cent, is fixed by the Treasury. The interest is payable gross and is recoverable as a debt due to the Crown – by distraint if necessary. It is not allowable as a deduction but if tax on which interest has been paid becomes refundable as an overcharge the interest is refundable also. Interest is chargeable from a RECKONABLE DATE, which depends on the nature of the income assessed (that is, which Schedule it falls under); it is not charged, however, on income assessable on a remittance basis if because of, say, exchange restrictions that income cannot be remitted and ceases from the date the Board first knew the relevant facts.

(b) *Paid.* See LOAN INTEREST.

(c) *Received* (and see BANK INTEREST).

Generally interest is receivable gross although there are circumstances in which tax is deducted (see DEDUCTION OF TAX) or deemed to be deducted as in the case of BUILDING SOCIETY or BANK INTEREST. The assessment is under Schedule D, Case III (or Cases IV and V if the interest is from abroad) on the PREVIOUS YEAR BASIS.

Some items of interest are exempt. They include interest on sums received for damages or death, on certain British Government stocks held by non-residents, on the first £70 of ordinary National Savings Bank interest, on SAVINGS CERTIFICATES and on overpaid tax (see above).

Special provisions relate to the interest element in deep discount securities and indexed stock.

Interviews. A taxpayer may wish to discuss his tax affairs but find that his DISTRICT is a LONDON PROVINCIAL DISTRICT. He can arrange for his file to be sent to an ENQUIRY OFFICE or, if there is not one convenient, to the DISTRICT nearest his home.

Intestacy. This means dying without leaving a will. The residuary estate devolves according to the Administration of Estates Act, 1925, and the Intestates' Estate Act, 1952: the surviving spouse takes all the personal chattels absolutely, £40,000 (£85,000 if no issue) free of death duties and a life interest in half the rest of the estate. The other half of the residue and the reversionary interest is held on the statutory trusts for the children and grandchildren. The statutory trusts are for all the children of the intestate living at his death and attain 18 or marry, in equal shares. Different considerations apply if the intestate leaves no children or grandchildren, but leaves a parent, brother or sister or leaves no spouse but children or grandchildren.

There may be partial intestacy where a will validly disposes of only part of the property so the balance continues as an intestacy.

Invalid car allowance. Disabled persons' vehicle maintenance grants under the 1977 National Health Service Act are not taxable.

Investigation. An omnibus term arising out of the need for the INSPECTOR OF TAXES to be satisfied with a return of income. If he is not satisfied he must make an assessment to the best of his judgement: and that judgement may well need considerable investigation before it can be exercised. Investigation may be a simple enquiry into, say, the source of some capital; on the other hand it may be a painstaking exercise over a long period into an elaborate fraud. It may be a few questions from the district; it may involve a prolonged examination by Enquiry Branch. The onus is always on the taxpayer to displace the Revenue's assessments. (See AUDIT, ENQUIRY BRANCH, FRAUD, IN-DEPTH PROCEDURE, NEGLECT, SPECIAL OFFICE, WILFUL DEFAULT.)

Investment income surcharge. A surcharge of 15 per cent levied on investment income exceeding £7,100 in 1983/84. This was the last year the tax was levied; it was abolished from 1984/85.

J

Job related living accommodation. Living accommodation provided by the employer for the employee by reason of his employment, or for his wife, by reason of hers, where:

(a) the employee needs to live in the accommodation to perform properly the duties of his employment;
(b) he needs to live in the accommodation to perform the duties better than he would if he did not;
(c) there is a special threat to the employer's security and the employee occupies the accommodation as part of the security arrangements;
(d) there is a commercial contract requiring the employee or his wife to carry on a trade or live on premises provided by another person.

The above conditions must apply for the benefit not to be assessable. Note that (a) and (b) do not apply when the director of a company is involved.

Job severance payments. See COMPENSATION FOR LOSS OF OFFICE.

Journalists' expenses. A somewhat touchy subject, so mentioning El Vino to the Revenue is not considered tactful. But expenses of a journalist such as supplying himself with essential reference books, renewal of a typewriter or even in some cases use of home as an office may qualify. It is likely in the case of the last two that the journalist is freelance and therefore assessable under Schedule D, Case II when more liberal criteria for expenses will apply.

K

Keith Committee. A Committee set up in 1980 to consider the enforcement powers of the BOARDS OF INLAND REVENUE and CUSTOMS AND EXCISE. It reported in four volumes between 1983 and 1985. The general thrust of the recommendations was away from discretion and more towards fixed PENALTIES, a policy already emphasised in the new penalty code for VAT. The draft proposals for revised income tax penalties have been published. (See *The Inland Revenue and The Taxpayer,* HMSO, December, 1986).

Keyman insurance. Policies taken out by companies on the life of key personnel. If the policy proceeds go to the company, they are taxable as trading receipts and the premium paid may be claimed as allowable expenses. Otherwise they are treated as capital receipts and payments respectively.

L

Life assurance premium relief. Tax relief given on premiums payable on a QUALIFYING POLICY, now given by deduction from the premium. The relief is not available for insurances made after March 13, 1984, nor is relief given for policies made before that date if the policy is varied so as to secure increased benefits. Relief by deduction dates from 1979/80; the insurance company recovers the difference from the Inland Revenue. For many years the relief has been restricted to 15 per cent of the premiums paid subject to an overriding limit of £1,500 or one sixth of TOTAL INCOME, whichever is the greater. Special rules apply in determining whether a policy qualifies, the most important being that the normal term must exceed ten years.

Limited partnership. A limited partner is a partner carrying on a trade; but he is still assessable under Schedule D. He may be:

(a) a limited partner in a partnership registered under the 1907 Limited Partnership Act;
(b) a general partner in a partnership but not responsible for management or for debts or obligations contracted for trade purposes;
(c) a person who, under any overseas law, is not responsible for management or trade liabilities. See SALARIED PARTNER.

Lloyd's underwriters. See UNDERWRITERS.

Loan interest relief. Interest on loans paid at a reasonable commercial rate qualifies for relief if:

(a) it is annual interest chargeable under Schedule D, Case III in the recipient's hands;
(b) it is payable on a loan from a UK bank in the UK, or from a bank or finance house carrying on business in the UK or from a member of the stock exchange;
(c) the loan to which it relates has been used for a qualifying purpose within a reasonable time of being taken out.

The qualifying purposes are as follows.

(a) Buying or improving land or buildings in the UK and the Irish Republic.
(b) Acquiring an interest in a CLOSE COMPANY.
(c) Acquiring an interest in a cooperative or a partnership.
(d) An employee acquiring shares in an employee-run company.
(e) Paying capital transfer tax.
(f) Buying, in certain circumstances, a life annuity.
(g) Buying machinery or plant by partners or employees.

There are limits and conditions attaching to the relief in each case. Qualifying interest is deductible in the year of assessment in which the interest is paid. There is a ceiling on the amount of the loan under (a) above on which the interest qualifies for relief; but interest on a BRIDGING LOAN also qualifies for relief in addition to interest paid on an existing mortgage. If the bridging loan is made by the employer it may exceed the limit if: the loan is not in excess of the market value of the old property; it is completely repaid when that is sold; it is outstanding for only twelve months; and used only to pay off the old mortgage or the new property cost. (See MIRAS.)

London Provincial Districts. Set up in various provincial cities – Manchester, Bradford, Middlesborough, Gateshead, Glasgow and Edinburgh, for example – as well as Cardiff and Liverpool (although the districts themselves have other names) to deal with Schedule E liabilities which could not be dealt with in London because of the difficulty of recruiting suitable staff.

Long service testimonial awards. The award of shares (on or after March 12, 1984) or of tangible articles to any employee, for service of 20 years or more, is exempt from tax provided the cost to the employer does not exceed £20 for each year of service and no similar award had been made to the recipient within the previous ten years.

Lorry driver, subsistence allowances. An employee engaged as a driver may have no fixed area of work if he is travelling full-time while performing his duties. There is a STATEMENT OF PRACTICE which deals with the extra cost of meals away from home. There is now no restriction by the Revenue for the element of 'home saving'.

Luncheon vouchers. These are exempted by concession up to a value of 15p per working day. If the vouchers supplied to an employee exceed this limit, only the excess is taxed.

M

Maintenance and education. Where, under a UK court order, payment is made to any person under 21 for his maintenance, benefit or education or to someone else for the maintenance and so on of a person under 18, then, subject to certain limits, the payments are made gross and the recipient, if liable, is charged to tax under Schedule D, Case III.

The matter also and more commonly arises in relation to payments from a trust, and covers reasonable provision out of the income from settled property, taking into account the age and needs of the infant beneficiary and the general circumstances of the case. (See also HUSBAND AND WIFE and SMALL MAINTENANCE PAYMENTS.) Any other payments must be made under deduction of income tax at the basic rate, so as to constitute taxed income in the recipient's hands.

Maintenance payment. A payment made by a partner in a marriage by way of provision to the other partner or for a child of both or either of the partners, or a payment to provide for a child made by his natural father.

Market value. For capital gains purposes in relation to any assets, market value means the price that these assets might reasonably be expected to fetch on a sale in the open market. Generally the term is taken to mean the price arrived at between a willing buyer and a willing seller on a commercial basis. See AT ARM'S LENGTH.

Marriage, tax consequences of. See HUSBAND AND WIFE.

Medical insurance. For lower paid employees, this is not taxable. For HIGHER PAID EMPLOYEES, the cost to the employer is taxable. If it is taken out, as it commonly is, for a group of employees, each is taxable on a proportion of the cost on a just and reasonable basis, less any contribution from the employee. The benefit, however, is not taxable when the insurance is against the cost of medical treatment abroad while the employee is performing the duties of his office. As far as actual medical treatment paid for by the employer is concerned, this would normally be regarded as an assessable benefit.

MIRAS. See MORTGAGE INTEREST RELIEF AT SOURCE.

Moonlighting. An aspect of the hidden or BLACK ECONOMY and generally taken to mean a full-time or part-time job not declared to the Revenue and totally separate from any normal occupation which might be declared and therefore subjected to PAYE. The term certainly reflects the clandestine, often nocturnal, activity which it usually is. There are no convincing figures of its prevalence.

Mortgage interest relief at source (MIRAS). After April 5, 1983, mortgage interest on home loans is generally paid after deduction of tax at the basic rate if the interest is relevant loan interest, paid by a qualifying borrower to a qualifying lender. Tax relief at the higher rates will continue to be given in Schedule E codings and other assessments.

A relevant loan interest is defined as an interest which became due after April 5, 1983 and is paid to a *qualifying lender* (see below) and is on loans for the purchase or improvement of land, caravan or house boat in the UK used as the only or main residence of the borrower. A *qualifying borrower* is an individual who pays relevant loan interest unless his emoluments are free of tax under, say, diplomatic immunity. A qualifying lender may be a bank, a building society, a local authority, the Bank of England, the Post Office, insurance companies, a trustee savings bank, a friendly society, and so on.

Motor car. The provision of a company car is still one of the most tax-efficient perks and for a lower paid employee it is free of tax. For a higher paid employee who makes private use of a car, the amount of benefit assessable is set out in arbitrary scales; the Revenue recognised some years ago that it was impossible to ensure that all such employees paid the correct amount of tax on the benefit. The legislation from 1976 onwards, therefore, tried to simplify the problem by introducing a system of flat-rate benefits.

There is now a scale charge which is uprated annually and is related to the cubic capacity of the car and whether it is more or less than four years old. Cars costing over £16,000 currently are rated by cubic capacity and have a higher scale attached to them. There is a similar scale charge for petrol. For more detailed treatment, see CAR.

The tabular figures are reduced if the employee makes a contribution towards costs: if, for instance, the employee pays all his own petrol, the petrol scale charge will be nil. Where the mileage exceeds 18,000 for business purposes, the car scale charge is halved: where it is less than 2,500 both scales are increased by a half: in such a case it would be better for the employee to buy his own petrol and avoid the petrol scale charge.

In fact, with the continuing increase in scale charges, an INSUBSTANTIAL BUSINESS USER might be better advised to claim business mileage according to the AA mileage rates than be provided with a company car. The Revenue, however, is reluctant to adopt AA mileage rates because they contain an element of depreciation.

Musician. This entry (see also JOURNALIST) may be taken as a model for other employments which have a professional flavour. The operation of PAYE is, of course, the same for all employees; it is the expenses which make the difference for a professional person whether musician, singer, dancer or actor (although the last three are more usually assessed under Schedule D). A musician can often legitimately claim such items as insurance of his instrument or its replacement, taxi fares after late-night sessions when public transport is not available. But it is essential to keep careful records; the Revenue is much more sympathetic when this is systematically done.

N

National insurance contributions. Class 4 national insurance contributions from 1985/86 onwards may be claimed as a deduction of 50 per cent of the amount (as finally determined) for the year of assessment. There is an elaborate table which gives the various contributions for the four classes of national insurance contributions.

Neglect. One of the three categories (see FRAUD and WILFUL DEFAULT) which attract penalties under any of the Taxes Acts but it is the least serious of the three. The statutory definition is 'negligence or failure to give any notice, make any return or to produce or furnish any document or information required by or under the Taxes Act'.

Net related earnings. These are significant in determining the maximum amount of RETIREMENT ANNUITY premiums a self-employed individual may pay in one year. They are defined as the amount of an individual's RELEVANT EARNINGS for the year of assessment, less deductions such as losses and capital allowance.

Newspaper industry, casual employees. There was some adverse publicity on this matter when casual employees were evading tax by giving false and often comic names. An amnesty for back tax was declared and a special scheme introduced by which such payments were taxed at the basic rate and centralised in a special London Provincial District.

Nominee directors. If company A has the right to nominate directors of company B to represent its interests, such directors are nominee directors; their fees may be paid gross and included in company A's corporation tax computation.

Non-cash vouchers. Generally defined as any voucher, stamp or similar document capable of being exchanged for money's worth, goods or services. With effect from April 6, 1982, the definition of non-cash vouchers was extended to a so-called cheque voucher, which may be used by an employee to pay for particular goods or services. The receipt of these vouchers is treated for tax purposes as an emolument equal to the expense incurred of providing them.

Notice of assessment. See ASSESSMENT, NOTICE OF.

Notice of coding. Tax codes regulate the deduction of tax from earnings and represent the total allowances less the final digit. Once the Inspector has determined the code for a taxpayer he issues a notice of coding if there is a change from the preceding year; the employer will also be notified if there is any change. Codes have suffixes, various letters of the alphabet, which enable employers to give quick effect to Budget changes: for example, H (higher personal allowance); L (lower personal allowance); T requires a further notification from the inspector; P (single age allowance); V (married age allowance); D (higher rates of tax applicable). Appeals against codings are made to the GENERAL COMMISSIONERS.

Notification of liability. Formal assessments may be made under Schedule E to test the accuracy of the deductions (see NOTICE OF CODING). Repayments are dealt with by a payable order issued at the same time as the notice of assessment; under-payments are usually taken into account in the next or next but one coding and so collected over a period. Formal assessments, however, are not made when the coding and tax deducted are correct, although it is open to any taxpayer to request an assessment: notice must be given within five years after the end of the year of assessment. (See also ASSESSMENT, NOTICE OF.)

Nursery facilities. By concession nurseries subsidised by employers for periods up to April 5, 1985, were not taxed, but from that date on they are liable to tax as a BENEFIT IN KIND by HIGHER PAID EMPLOYEES but not lower paid ones.

O

Objections and appeals. The only way of challenging an assessment properly is by the process of appeal: note also that the appeal procedure extends to any formal decision by an INSPECTOR or the BOARD OF INLAND REVENUE such as a refusal to grant a relief. An appeal must normally be made within 30 days of the date of the NOTICE OF ASSESSMENT but there is a late appeal procedure. The inspector may admit a late appeal; if he does not, the COMMISSIONERS may. An appeal cannot be withdrawn except by written agreement on both sides, and the Commissioners have no statutory power to recall a determination; the Lord Chancellor has, however, given them discretion to do so if they consider there is good and sufficient reason. Otherwise their decision stands unless one of the parties expresses DISSATISFACTION and asks for a CASE STATED for the opinion of the High Court.

Obtained by reason of employment. This phrase relates to BENEFITS IN KIND and in particular to the Schedule E charge on interest-free loans. Where a loan is made by the person's employer, the benefit is regarded as obtained by reason of employment if the loan was made by a company over which the employer had control directly or indirectly. Where the employer is an individual and the loan can be shown to have been made in the normal course of his domestic, family or personal relationships, no benefit arises. See BENEFICIAL LOAN ARRANGEMENTS.

Office. The classic definition of an 'office' handed down by the Courts is 'a subsisting, permanent, substantive position, which had an existence independent of the person who filled it, and which went on and was filled in succession by successive holders'; it was not until 1922 that offices were finally brought under Schedule E. The word covers four columns in the New English Dictionary but the most apposite has been thought to be: 'a position or place to which certain duties are attached, especially one of a more or less public character'.

Official error, remission of tax in case of. Where arrears of tax have arisen, the Revenue may admit responsibility for not having made proper and timely use of returns and information supplied, so that the taxpayer could reasonably assume his affairs were in order. The Revenue will then repay a proportion of the tax. This proportion is determined by the gross amount of the taxpayer's income; these income limits have been revised from time to time since 1971 when this particular concession was introduced. No remission is granted where the taxpayer's total income exceeds £23,000 (£25,000 for pensioners and individuals aged over 65).

The Board of Inland Revenue has always operated a remission of tax policy on the grounds of poverty, equity, cost-effectiveness of pursuit or plain inability to collect, when, say, a taxpayer disappears abroad. This, like error remission, is non-statutory but is covered by the Board's general care and management powers.

Offshore funds. A complex subject concerned with non-resident trusts whose position was substantially modified by the 1984 legislation. Briefly, offshore income gains which are judged to have been insufficiently distributed (see below) will be charged to income tax or corporation tax under Schedule D, Case VI, not capital gains tax. That will only apply to any part of such gain arising before January 1, 1984, but the whole of the subsequent gain will be taxed as income: indexation will not apply. There are special provisions to enable funds to satisfy the *distribution test* – broadly that 85 per cent of the funds' income is distributed.

Ombudsman. His statutory title is the Parliamentary Commissioner for Administration and his function is to look into alleged cases of maladministration by government departments including the Inland Revenue and Customs and Excise. He can only be approached through an MP and only then when all the normal remedies have failed. Although the Revenue is usually top of the complaints league with some 40–50 cases a year, among 25 million potential complaint cases to quote one Chairman of the Board of Inland Revenue, the percentage may be regarded as small.

Only or main residence. In the context of relief for LOAN INTEREST this is defined as the taxpayer's principal or more important residence. Some relief is also allowed where the individual does not live in the house because his employment requires him to live elsewhere.

Options and shares. See APPROVED SHARE OPTION SCHEMES.

Ordinarily resident. For tax purposes the status of a taxpayer has to be decided for a tax year. Hence there is nothing immediately difficult about the concept of being ordinarily resident; it means habitually resident or residence which is not casual or uncertain but in the ordinary course of a person's life. In theory a person could be ordinarily resident if he was overseas on holiday for over twelve months; a person could also be RESIDENT but not ordinarily resident if he lived overseas but spent more than 183 days in this country in a particular tax year.

But if a person comes from overseas to work and intends to remain for more than two years he would be regarded as resident from the outset, and ordinarily resident as well if he intended to remain for three years or more. Otherwise a person coming with no such clear intention is regarded as ordinarily resident when it is obvious that he intends to remain for three or more years and has AVAILABLE ACCOMMODATION. Visits to this country averaging three months or more for four consecutive years by an individual, even where there is no available accommodation, would also be held to constitute ordinary residence.

Overpayment. When an assessment has been made which shows that a repayment is due, the full amount is usually repaid without application; where the repayment is £5 or less an assessment will not be made.

Overrepayments of tax. Tax overrepaid after April 5 is refundable to the Revenue and recoverable by assessment as if it were tax unpaid; the assessment would include any excess repayment supplement. The time limit for such an assessment can be extended to six years after the end of the chargeable period following that in which the overpayment was made.

Overseas customers. Expenditure on BUSINESS ENTERTAINMENT for overseas customers is allowable; for this purpose, they are defined as follows:

(a) any person not ordinarily resident in the UK or carrying on a trade there, who avails himself, or who may be expected to avail himself, in the course of a trade carried on by him outside the UK, of any goods, facilities or services which it is the trade of the UK trader to provide;
(b) any person not ordinarily resident in the UK who acts, in relation to such goods, facilities or services, on behalf of an overseas customer within (a) or on behalf of any government or public authority of a country outside the UK.

Overseas emoluments. Defined as those of a person not domiciled in the UK from an employer not resident in the UK; the non-resident status can be maintained even if there is an agency in this country liable to UK income tax. No Schedule E, Case I liability arises but there is liability under Case III. (See SCHEDULE E, Cases I, II and III) where the duties are performed wholly abroad. Where they are performed wholly or partly in the UK all three schedules may apply. See FOREIGN EMOLUMENTS.

P

Pamphlets. See BOARD'S PAMPHLETS and list on p. 116.

P11D (1985). This is the statutory form which an EMPLOYER is required to complete every year for each DIRECTOR or HIGHER PAID EMPLOYEE giving details of expenses reimbursed to, or paid on behalf of, the individuals, and of all benefits (for example, car, accommodation, cheap loans) and other facilities provided to the individuals or members of their families. This information provides the Revenue with the basis of assessing the BENEFITS IN KIND of the individual.

P45. When an employee leaves, the employer must prepare a form P45. This is in three parts attached so that certain entries in parts 2 and 3 are copies of part 1. The certificate includes all the relevant details concerning the employee, his total gross pay to date and the total tax deducted. Part 1 of the form is then sent to the Inspector of Taxes; parts 2 and 3 are given to the employee to hand to his new employer.

P60. This form must be completed annually by the employer and handed to each employee. It shows details of the year's remuneration and the tax deducted.

Parties. The Revenue is on record as saying that it will not seek tax on 'modest expenditure' on Christmas and office parties generally open to the staff. 'Modest' is defined around £30 to £35 a head annually, so it might be difficult to have a Christmas party and, say, a staff summer outing. No P11D will be called for if this limit is not exceeded. Nothing has ever been said about indexing.

Partnerships. The relevance of partnership to Schedule E arises when there is a question whether a so-called partner is really acting as such or whether he is a SALARIED PARTNER and therefore in tax terms an EMPLOYEE. It is also a point to consider when a self-employed person is paying wages to his wife. The level of remuneration may be geared to avoiding NIC and so may not be an adequate reward. If in fact she is concerned in the administration of the business, then thought should be given to a partnership when the problems both of NIC and a challenge from the Revenue are more easily solved.

Part-time public appointments. Professional persons who hold part-time public appointments are assessable under Schedule E on the remuneration so derived, although the fees from other outside appointments, if not considerable, can be included in their Schedule D, Case II assessment. See ACCOUNTANTS, DENTISTS and DOCTORS.

Paye As You Earn (PAYE). See below.

PAYE. A method of deducting tax from all emoluments assessable under Schedule E. It was introduced in 1943 to cope with the explosion in wage earners that followed the Second World War. Previously, except in the case of civil servants, tax had been paid by direct assessments as with tax assessable under Schedule D.

Each PAYE taxpayer is given a code number (see NOTICE OF CODING) which regulates the amount of tax to be deducted from his remuneration either on a weekly or a monthly basis by his employer. The employer refers to PAYE tax tables which enable him to work out the deductions, on a cumulative basis, so that they as nearly as possible equal the total tax liability from the previous April 6.

National insurance contributions are also deducted at the same time (see DEDUCTIONS WORKING SHEET). It is, however, possible for some items such as pensions to be assessed directly, as the tax is demanded quarterly. This is known as 'direct collection'.

The tax and contributions thus deducted must be paid to the COLLECTOR within 14 days after the end of each month, and proper operation of the system is monitored by the PAYE Audit branch which has the right of inspection. At the end of the year the employer must hand in to the Revenue:

An end of year return (P14).
A declaration on form P35.
A deductions working sheet for each employee (P11 (new)).
Details of payments relating to a different year and emoluments not in cash (P90).
Forms P11D for all directors and higher paid employees giving details of expenses and so on.

Each employee must also be provided with a form (P60) showing his total taxable emoluments for the year and the tax paid. Penalties may be imposed for non-compliance with the PAYE regulations. It has been held that the employer is not entitled to charge the Board of Inland Revenue with the cost of acting as an unpaid Collector of Taxes. See AUDIT, PAYE.

Paying agent. A person (other than the National Debt Commissioners or the Bank of England or the Bank of Ireland which pay interest on government stock) who is entrusted with the payment of dividends out of the public revenue of any government and the revenue of any public authority or institution outside the UK. It also includes a banker in the UK who sells or otherwise realises coupons, and a dealer in coupons in the UK who purchases coupons. The agent must deduct tax at basic rate; this is then charged on him under Schedule C and payable within 30 days from the issue of the notice of assessment.

Pecuniary liability of employee borne by employer. As a general rule if an employee receives money or money's worth from his employer he is chargeable to tax on that amount. There are, however, certain exceptions, where the employer is liable, such as services and accommodation related to the duties, provision of pensions, canteen meals, travelling expenses between companies by a director of each, removal expenses, miners' free coal, LUNCHEON VOUCHERS, MEDICAL INSURANCE in certain circumstances and Christmas PARTIES. It would exclude any payment made by the employer as an individual made in the normal course of a domestic, family or personal relationship.

Peel, Sir Robert. Prime minister in 1842 when he decided to reimpose income tax, 'that mighty engine', as he called it, at a rate of 7d in the pound (1.9 per cent) in order to subsidise the free trade movement. He, not his chancellor, launched the Budget speech, with the interesting assumption that the tax would only be required 'for a time to be limited'. He was wise enough not to define what that limit might be.

Penalties. Broadly, there are two types of penalty provided for in the income tax Acts: penalties for errors of omission and penalties for errors of commission. In the first category is the failure to make a return of income for which the penalty is £50. If the failure continues into the next year of assessment the tax on the unreturned income is added to the penalty; this can be avoided if the failure is made good before proceedings start. For failure to make special returns including certificates, statements or other documents when required to do so, the penalty is £50 plus a daily penalty of £10 after judgment by the Court or Commissioners unless again the failure is remedied before proceedings can be taken.

Errors of commission are more severely penalised. For negligently (see NEGLIGENCE) or fraudulently (see FRAUD) submitting an incorrect return the maximum penalties are £50 plus the amount of tax underpaid in the case of negligence and £50 plus twice the amount of tax underpaid in the case of fraud. On special returns, if one is made negligently the maximum penalty is £250, if fraudulently, £500.

There are other miscellaneous penalty provisions. For assisting in the making of an incorrect return the penalty is £500; this would apply to an agent. For unlawful dealings with a subcontractor in the construction industry the maximum fine is £5,000. There is lastly the penalty for not giving notice of chargeability, up to £100.

The Board of Inland Revenue has, however, the power to mitigate penalties and it is now well known that the procedure – except where a decision has been taken to prosecute – is to take 100 per cent of the tax on omissions and then mitigate it by up to 40 per cent for cooperation, 20 per cent for disclosure, and 40 per cent for gravity.

The whole question of penalties was considered by the KEITH COMMITTEE and it may be in the future there will be a tendency more to fixed penalties as with value added tax and less to discretion.

The time limit for the start of proceedings to recover penalties is within six years after the date on which the penalty was incurred. It can be extended beyond that period where fraud or wilful default has been committed. See PENALTY PROCEEDINGS; PRECEPT.

Penalty proceedings. Where there has been failure to make a return, penalty proceedings may be begun by the Inspector before the General Commissioners. Otherwise they would be initiated by the Board of Inland Revenue and can be taken by way of appeal successively to the High Court, the Court of Appeal and the House of Lords.

Pensions. Within the charge to Schedule E and include pensions paid voluntarily and capable of being discontinued. Pensions received from various colonial pension funds by individuals resident in the UK are exempt.

Pension schemes. Contributions to secure pensions are variously treated: social security contributions are not allowed as a deduction for tax purposes to an individual; they are allowable to a business employer when paid in respect of an employee. Superannuation fund deductions are, however, allowable against an employee's Schedule E liability, and normally given automatic deduction through the PAYE system. See also APPROVED PENSION SCHEMES.

Personal and domestic employees. If the wages of such employees exceed the tax threshold, the employer will need to operate a PAYE scheme. But the expense of employing a domestic servant to enable a wife to go to work or a nurse to look after young children for a widower also to go out to work has been held not to be admissible as a deduction for an employer.

Personal reliefs. See ALLOWANCES.

Pitt, William, the Younger. In 1799 Pitt realised that he could no longer finance the campaign against Napoleon with an ill-regulated expenditure tax and made the momentous decision to introduce income tax. It was in fact repealed in 1802 and reintroduced by Addington in a very different form. But Pitt deserves the credit for shattering the Englishman's instinctive and traditional resistance to direct taxation. The fiscal scene could never be the same again.

Poinding. The Scots equivalent of DISTRAINT.

Pooled car. This is a car which the inspector is satisfied:

(a) that in the year concerned, it was made available to and actually used by more than one of the employees (of one or more employers) and, in the case of each, it was made available to him by reason of his employment and it was not (in that year) ordinarily used by any one of them to the exclusion of the others; and

(b) for any one of them the private use was merely incidental; and

(c) it was not in that year normally left overnight in or near premises where any of the employees was residing, except while being kept overnight on premises occupied by the person making the car available to them.

See also CAR.

Possessions. This word is used in the charging section of Schedule D, Case V and means all sources of income other than securities. It includes maintenance received by a divorced woman resident in the UK from a non-resident former husband and an annuity paid to a married woman resident in the UK by her separated husband under a foreign deed of separation.

Precept. A notice (the word precept is not now used in the TAXES MANAGEMENT ACT) which may be given by the COMMISSIONERS at any time before the determination of an appeal to the appellant or other party to the proceedings (but not to an Inspector) requiring him to deliver certain information within a specified time. There is a penalty for non-compliance. The information thus obtained is made available to the Revenue. There are also limited provisions for obtaining information from a third party.

Prerogative orders. This rather formidable and legalistic phrase covers for fiscal purposes the three writs mentioned below. They can be applied for by a taxpayer from the High Court to prevent inferior courts or officials from exceeding their powers or not exercising those powers in accordance with the law. There are two basic points to bear in mind.

(a) Such remedies cannot be sought until all the other normal processes of law have been exhausted.

(b) Expert legal advice will be necessary where it is considered application for any of these orders is appropriate.

These are the writs.

Mandamus ('we order'). A demand by the High Court ordering an inferior court or person to perform a duty appropriate to their office.
Prohibition. The opposite of *mandamus*, in that it orders an inferior court not to exceed its jurisdiction.

Certiorari ('to make more certain'). Enables the court to review the decision of an inferior court and to decide whether it has exceeded its powers or acted contrary to the rules of natural justice.

There is a long line of tax cases which shows that these remedies must not be resorted to until all the other available avenues of relief have been tried and found wanting.

Press releases. In this context, the explanations of Revenue practice which are issued from time to time, and especially after the Budget. Some are eventually reissued as STATEMENTS OF PRACTICE. Copies of any press release may be obtained from Inland Revenue, Public Enquiry Room, Somerset House, London WC2R 1LB.

Pretrading expenditure. A Schedule E taxpayer who is thinking of setting up on his own account but is testing the commercial waters by incurring preliminary expenditure is able, since March 31, 1980, to claim relief for this when incurred in the three years before he actually started to trade, provided it ranks as expenditure which would have been allowable had he been trading. Such expenditure is treated in the same way as a loss incurred in the first year of trading.

Previous year basis. The normal basis of assessment for Schedule D whereby the income, profits or gains are charged to tax on the basis of the amounts arising in the year preceding the year of assessment – that is, any accounts ending on any date between April 6, 1987, and April 5, 1988, form the basis of the assessment for 1988/89.

Prize incentive schemes. See AWARDS.

Profession. A person has been held by the Courts to be exercising a profession when his activities demand purely intellectual skill or manual skill directed by intellectual skill as in the case of a painter or sculptor. From a tax point of view, if an author or artist also holds an appointment, he will be assessed separately on his emoluments under Schedule E; if, however, the emoluments are small and the appointment more casual, it may be administratively more convenient to include such earnings in a Schedule D, Case II computation. (See VOCATION, DENTISTS, DOCTORS.)

Professional bodies, learned societies. Deductions are allowable where the annual subscription for membership of the relevant society is a condition of the employment and the society is one established for the advancement of knowledge, the spreading of good practice and so on. The Board of Inland Revenue approves a list of such bodies, which is regularly updated and this is available, price currently £3.50, from Inland Revenue Library, Room 8, New Wing, Somerset House, London WC2R 1LB.

Profit sharing schemes. There is no Schedule E charge on the appropriation of shares under an approved scheme provided that:

(a) the scheme does not possess any features which are neither essential nor reasonably incidental to the purpose of providing for directors' and employees' benefits in the nature of interests in shares;
(b) the participating employees are resident in the UK;
(c) out of monies paid to them by the company, the employees are required by the scheme to purchase appropriate shares in the employing company (or another group company);
(d) the company appropriates the shares so purchased to individuals who participate in the scheme provided they are eligible;
(e) the scheme is operated through a properly constituted trust;
(f) the scheme provides that the total of the initial market value of the shares appropriated to any one participant in a year of assessment will not exceed the lesser of £5,000 and 10 per cent of his salary but with a lower limit in any case of £1,250.

For shares disposed of after July 24, 1985, the charge to tax is:

Before fourth anniversary of allotment,	100 per cent
On or after fourth anniversary, but before fifth,	75 per cent
After fifth anniversary,	no charge

For employees who leave the company the charge is 50 per cent. See also BONUS.

Property, income from. Income from property is assessed under Schedule A (but see also FURNISHED LETTING), which applies to profits or gains arising from rent and other duties arising from land and buildings and any other receipts. Deductions are allowed for maintenance and repairs, landlord's services generally, rates, insurance, wages, accountancy fees and legal fees for preparing leases if for not more than 21 years. Premiums on leases are also chargeable to tax by the recipient, where the lease does not exceed 50 years. Liability is based on treating the premium as additional rent receivable at the date the lease was granted less one fiftieth for each full year less one in the lease's duration: for example, if it was a 25 year lease 26/50 of the premium would be chargeable. The balance of the premium not charged to income tax in this way is subject to capital gains tax.

The assessment is made on the profit arising in the previous tax year, adjustable to actual profit when the exact figures are known. Tax is due on January 1 in the year of assessment. If the Schedule A assessment is small and consistent in amount it may be possible to have the recipient's PAYE coding adjusted to save the inconvenience of a small separate assessment. Tax is due from the recipient of the rents but if he does not pay, the burden falls on the lessee who can deduct the tax from his payments of rent.

Purchased life annuity. The capital element in such annuities is not taxable because it is not treated as income to the purchaser. This applies to any annuity, whatever the conditions, purchased from a person dealing in life annuities. Loan interest relief is available for the purchase of a life annuity for a borrower aged 65 or over, where he borrows on the security of his house; the amount that ranks for interest relief in this way is limited to £30,000.

Q

Qualifying period. The 100 per cent deduction from remuneration for absences abroad is available to an employee if in any year of assessment the duties are performed wholly or partly outside the UK during a qualifying period. This must fall partly or wholly in the year of assessment and consist of at least 365 consecutive days. Short intervening periods spent in the UK will be ignored provided there are no more than 62 intervening days and the total of all time spent in the UK does not exceed one sixth of the whole period up to the next visit.

Qualifying policy. Basically qualifying policies may be divided into four categories.

(a) *Endowment policies.* The life assessed must be either that of the policyholder or spouse, its duration must be at least ten years, premiums must be payable at least once a year, and must not exceed twice the premiums paid in any other year or one eighth of the total premiums which would be payable if the policy ran for its full term.

(b) *Whole life policy and term assurance where death or disability is not restricted to within ten years.* Here again the life assured must be either that of the policyholder or spouse and the premiums must be payable at least once a year. Premiums are also payable until at least the life assured's death or disability or for ten years, and there are the same restrictions on amount of premiums payable over a twelve month period. The guaranteed sum payable on death must not be less than 75 per cent of the premiums payable if death occurred at 75 or up to date of cessation.

(c) *Term assurance where death or disability is restricted to within ten years.* The life assured must be that of the policyholder or spouse, the surrender value must not exceed the premiums paid, and there is the same 75 per cent minimum on the guaranteed sum payable at death or cessation.

(d) *Other life policies* such as industrial assurance policies, family income policies and mortgage protection policies are generally treated as qualifying policies even if the basic requirements are not fully met. (See LIFE ASSURANCE PREMIUM RELIEF.)

R

Receipts basis of assessment. Not a basis of assessment for Schedule E favoured by the Revenue but in practice the payments of remuneration in the year are so used when it is paid regularly weekly or monthly. Generally the Revenue prefers the EARNINGS BASIS or ACCOUNTS YEAR BASIS.

Reckonable date. In relation to interest on tax overdue, the reckonable date is:

(a) for any tax the date for the payment of which is laid down by the Taxes Management Act, 1970, S.55 and which, if there had been no APPEAL, would have become due and payable on an earlier date, that earlier date or the date in (c) below whichever is the later; and
(b) for any other tax charged by an assessment mentioned in Taxes Management Act, 1970, S.86(2) the date on which it became due and payable;
(c) the date referred to in (a) is the date on which the tax becomes due and payable or the date given in the table set out in the Taxes Management Act, 1970, S.86, whichever is the earlier.

None of the above is applicable to Schedule E taxed under PAYE.

Redundancy payment. A payment calculated in accordance with the Redundancy Payments Act, 1965. It should be paid by an employer to an employee who has been continuously employed for two years (currently) and who is either:

(a) dismissed by the employer by reason of redundancy; or
(b) laid-off or kept on short time to the extent specified in the Redundancy Payments Act, 1965, S.6(1) and complies with the requirements of that section.

It is not assessable to tax but needs to be taken into account with any other payments of COMPENSATION FOR LOSS OF OFFICE. But a payment to an employee under a non-statutory redundancy scheme may be taxable if it formed part of the employee's conditions of service or if there is an expectation of payment.

Reference number. An essential part of the Revenue's tracing system under Schedule E is the taxpayer's reference number, which must be quoted in all correspondence or the Revenue will not be able to

connect the form or the letter with the file as there is no sort of alphabetical index. It will be even more vital when the PAYE system has been computerised.

Regional controller. In 1976 the BOARD OF INLAND REVENUE introduced a regional organisation, consisting of 15 regions each in charge of a regional controller. He is responsible not only for the various DISTRICTS in his region but for the collection offices and PAYE audit centres. He would be the person to complain to failing satisfaction from the DISTRICT INSPECTOR. See COMPLAINTS, SYSTEM FOR.

Registered blind person. A person registered as a blind person in a register compiled under the National Assistance Act, 1948, S.29. See BLIND PERSON'S ALLOWANCE.

Regulation 29 determinations (PAYE). Where it seems to the Inspector that there may be PAYE tax due from the employer which has not been paid over to the Collector, he may determine the amount of the tax to the best of his judgement and inform the employer accordingly. The tax is treated as if the amount were income tax assessed on the employer. He can, of course, appeal against such an assessment.

Relevant earnings. The meaning of this phrase is important in relation to relief for RETIREMENT ANNUITY premiums. It comprises the following income chargeable to tax for the year of assessment in question.

(a) Income arising from an office or employment held by the individual other than a pensionable employment.
(b) Income from any property which forms part of the emoluments of any such office or employment held by the individual.

(c) Income which is chargeable under Schedule A, B or D and is immediately derived by an individual from the carrying on of a trade, profession or vocation either solely or in partnership.

(d) Income treated as earned income arising from patent rights.

Remittance basis. An individual not ORDINARILY RESIDENT in the UK is only assessable on emoluments arising from duties performed outside the UK on a remittance basis, the assessment being based on the amounts actually received in the UK that is, all income to which the taxpayer is legally entitled. Remittance also includes constructive remittance that is, the application of any income arising outside the UK towards the satisfaction of any debt or loan interest in the UK. Where, as often happens, the individual has a single contract of employment with duties partly here and partly overseas special consideration will need to be given to the application of the remittance basis to the overseas element of his emoluments. This is normally computed on a pro rata basis by reference to the days worked in the UK and those worked overseas in the tax year concerned.

Removal expenses borne by employer. Where the employee has to move house, either to change employment or on transfer within his organisation, removal expenses (including a temporary subsistence allowance while the employee is house hunting) paid by the employer, if reasonable and properly controlled, are not taxable as a benefit in kind.

Remuneration. See EARNED INCOME and EMOLUMENTS.

Repayment of tax. Many cases dealt with by the Revenue are labelled 'AR' – that is, automatic repayment. For example, if a taxpayer's income is wholly taxed at source, then the tax on the allowances due must be repaid. This is usually done annually; it may be half-yearly or even quarterly on request to the Inspector.

Repayment supplement. An amount payable by the Revenue as an increase in a tax repayment because of delay in making that repayment. It generally arises when repayment is made more than twelve months from the end of the year of assessment to which it relates; in the case of PAYE over-deductions it relates to the year of assessment in which deducted. The supplement is paid when the delayed repayment is £25 or more. It takes the form of a tax-free interest payment at varying rates (currently 9 per cent).

Residence. See ONLY OR MAIN RESIDENCE also HOUSE.

Residence abroad. For an individual whose DOMICILE is the UK, residence abroad is of practical significance when the individual wishes to claim the 100 per cent deduction for long absences abroad. He will be entitled to this deduction if the duties are performed wholly or partly outside the UK and any of them are performed in a QUALIFYING PERIOD which consists of at least 365 days.

Where an individual goes abroad and intends to remain abroad, he may be treated as not RESIDENT and not ORDINARILY RESIDENT from the date of leaving. He should have sold his home in the UK and the position will be reviewed after a complete tax year during which it is wise not to return to this country at all. His visits thereafter should not average more than three months annually. If he still has ACCOMMODATION AVAILABLE he will be treated as resident if he makes even one visit and ordinarily resident if he visits the UK for longer periods during his absence. (See RESIDENT and ORDINARILY RESIDENT.)

Resident. As far as an individual is concerned, he is regarded as being resident in the UK for any tax year if:

(a) he is physically present in the UK for six months or more in a tax year;
(b) if he makes a continuous series of visits to the UK for substantial (regarded as three months or more) periods;
(c) if he has AVAILABLE ACCOMMODATION in the UK;
(d) if he is a British subject resident in the UK.

Note that it is possible to be resident in any tax year in more than one country. If the question of residence becomes contentious it is a matter for the SPECIAL COMMISSIONERS.

Restrictive covenants. Where a sum is paid to an employee in return for an undertaking to restrict his activities in some way (for example, not to compete with his employers), the employee is assessable for the grossed up amount of the payment for the year in which the payment was made at higher rate with a credit for the notional basic rate tax added to the payment. Details of such payments must be forwarded to the Inspector by May 5 following the end of the year of assessment concerned.

Retainer. Held to fall within the general description of EMOLUMENTS of an office as it is of the same nature as 'salaries, fees, wages, perquisites and profits whatsoever'. The payment of a retainer would need to have some unusual conditions attached to it for there to be any question of non-assessability.

Retirement. Payments by an employer to a retirement benefits scheme which is a statutory scheme or a scheme approved by the Inland Revenue are not assessable on the employee: if, as is unlikely, either of those two conditions was not fulfilled, the contributions would be assessable on the employee. Where approval is not obtained and the payment is made under a scheme in which LIFE ASSURANCE PREMIUM RELIEF would be available to the individual, then such individual is entitled to that relief (this can only apply to schemes set up on or before March 13, 1984).

There are stringent conditions for approval which must normally be fully met although the Board of Inland Revenue has discretion to allow a scheme even if the terms are not fully complied with in every particular. When a scheme is approved, the employee's contribution is tax-deductible, and lump sums receivable on retirement are free of tax. The employer's contribution is allowable to him for tax purposes.

Retirement annuity. Available for employees not in pensionable employment (and for the self-employed). Within certain limits an individual may deduct from his RELEVANT EARNINGS any qualifying premium under a contract approved by the Inland Revenue.

The contract must have as its principal object the provision of a life annuity in old age and be made with a person carrying on a life annuity business in the UK. There must be no payment to the individual during his lifetime other than a life annuity payable to him after age 60 (though for certain professions where early retirement is the norm, an earlier age than 60 may be approved) and before age 75, and no payment after earlier death in service other than a life annuity to his wife or a tax free lump sum to his dependants. The limits to the relief are based on relevant earnings starting at 17.5 per cent and increasing with the age of the individual. Subject to certain conditions, premiums can be related back and unused relief carried forward.

Retirement or removal from office. See COMPENSATION FOR LOSS OF OFFICE and RETIREMENT.

Returns. Soon after the start of the tax year, income tax returns are issued to persons liable to tax. These in theory should be completed within 30 days but rarely are, which led the KEITH COMMITTEE to remark that the UK was a nation of non-compliers. Fortunately in practice further time is allowed and, in the case of Schedule E, returns are not issued every year to taxpayers whose only income is an employment so one should be requested if there are changes in allowances or reliefs.

The layout of returns has improved considerably over the past year or so and the accompanying notes are helpful and clear. The Board of Inland Revenue may impose PENALTIES if an assessment is delayed because of a late return; note that to write in any section 'to be forwarded later' or a similar form of words is not regarded as completing a return.

There are other returns which individuals and persons may be required to complete. (A person may be a company.) Returns are issued to persons in respect of income not their own which is chargeable to tax: bankers crediting interest without deduction of tax are required to make a return where (in practice and currently) the amount exceeds £150. EMPLOYERS have to make returns of EMPLOYEES' wages, salaries etc; payment of fees, commissions and royalties have to be returned by those who make them; issuing houses, stockbrokers and auctioneers have the duty of making returns when called upon to do so, as have trustees. Partnership returns must be completed by the precedent acting or principal partner, company returns by the 'proper office', normally the secretary. The Board of Inland Revenue has the power to prescribe the form of returns.

Rossminster. An omnibus title given to an avoidance industry which flourished in the 1970s fostered by two ingenious tax specialists called Roy Tucker and Ron Plummer (Rossminster was the name of their bank). The Revenue carried out a series of raids which, although not as successful as it had hoped, effectively put a stop to these activities. Their history has been chronicled by Nigel Tutt in *The Tax Raiders* (see TAX RAID).

Round sum allowances. DISPENSATION may be given by the Inspector where expense payments – for example, for travelling and subsistence – are not considered to give rise to any tax liability. Round sums rather than quantifiable amounts are normally excluded, but there are signs that the Revenue is taking a more relaxed view of these when they are clearly reasonable.

S

Salaried partner. The term may mean that the salary is regarded as that partner's share of the partnership profits and is, therefore, not allowable as a deduction in computing the firm's profits; he would be equally liable for tax under Schedule D as part of the partnership's tax liability but have a valid claim for interest on a loan to buy an interest in the partnership. He may, however, be virtually a salaried employee with no true partnership responsibilities. In this case, his salary would be deductible under Schedule D and assessable under Schedule E. The nature of the partner's relationship is the important factor not the actual label.

Savings certificates. The interest on national savings certificates issued under the National Loans Act, 1968, or the National Debt Act, 1958, or the 1920 Finance Act and any war savings certificates as defined in the National Debt Act, 1922, is exempt from tax. There are parallel enactments relating to Northern Ireland.

Savings-related share option schemes. Such schemes, first approved in 1980, are those in which an individual obtains a right to acquire shares in a company by reason of his position as a director or employee of that company. When such a scheme has been approved, no tax is chargeable on the receipt of the right to acquire shares, and, on exercising the right, no tax is chargeable in respect either of that exercise or of any increase in the market value of the shares. Currently the monthly contributions must not exceed £100 and the minimum is £10. The scheme must be linked to an approved savings scheme to provide the funds, when the option is exercised to buy the shares. See APPROVED SHARE OPTION SCHEMES.

SAYE share option scheme. See SAVINGS RELATED SHARE OPTION SCHEME.

Schedule A. Applies to property income other than furnished letting; this has applied since 1963. Originally Schedule A was charged on the net annual value of a property based on the rack rental less a statutory deduction for repairs.

Schedule B. Applies to the occupation of WOODLANDS in the UK managed on a commercial basis. The basis of assessment is one third of the annual value, which is determined as if the land were let in its natural and unimproved state; proceeds from the sale of timber are not chargeable to tax. There is an election for Schedule D assessment, with a two year time limit from the end of the year of assessment. This can be of advantage in the early years of occupation when the expenses of developing the woodlands exceed their revenue, so allowing losses to be claimed for tax purposes. The election once made is irrevocable so far as that occupier is concerned; however, on a change of occupier the Schedule D lapses and the Schedule B assessment is restored.

Schedule C. Applies to PAYING AGENTS on payment of interest, public annuities, dividends or shares of annuities out of the public revenue of any government and the revenue of any public authority or institution outside the UK. There are exemptions concerning limited UK Government Stocks.

Schedule D. Is divided into six sections or cases.

Case I: profits or gains of trades
Case II: profits or gains of professions or vocations
Case III: the taxation of INTEREST, ANNUITIES and ANNUAL PAYMENTS recoverable
Case IV: income from overseas securities
Case V: income from overseas possessions
Case VI: any annual profits or gains not falling under any other case of Schedule D and not charged by virtue of any other Schedule

Schedule E. Has three cases.

Case I: employment held by an individual resident and ordinarily resident in the UK
Case II: employment held by an individual not resident or, if resident, not ordinarily resident in the UK
Case III: employment held by an individual resident in the UK and not within Case I and II – for example, employees not domiciled in the UK receiving foreign emoluments where the duties are performed wholly abroad but the employee is resident and ordinarily resident in the UK.

Schedule F. This Schedule covers dividends and any other distributions received from a company resident in the UK.

With regard to the schedular system in general this was first instituted in 1803 by Addington to overcome the Englishman's natural reluctance to making a general return of income.

Scholarships. See EDUCATIONAL AND SCHOLARSHIP SCHEMES.

Seafarers. The duties of seafarers are deemed to be performed in the UK
if: the voyage does not extend to a port outside the UK; or the seafarer
is RESIDENT in the UK and either the voyage began or ended in the UK
or (with effect from April 4, 1984) it was a part of a voyage extending
to a port outside the UK. Standard PAYE procedure applies to seafarers
and travelling and subsistence allowances paid to a recipient who is
making regular voyages to the same UK port are treated as emoluments. There is a Marine Tax Deduction Scheme which regulates the
procedure, and in some cases the master of the ship may be treated as
the employer. If, however, a seafarer resident in the UK is away for a
full year of assessment he escapes tax for that year even if he has
ACCOMMODATION AVAILABLE. On the other hand, a seafarer who is not
resident may yet be liable to UK tax if he serves in the coasting trade.
The liability of airline pilots follows broadly the same principles.

Season tickets, transport vouchers. For higher paid employees these
were always taxable; for lower paid employees these have been generally taxable from April 6, 1982. The amount assessable is the cost to
the employer of providing such a voucher.

Self-administered pension schemes. Usually these must be for less
than twelve members and were developed because the conventional
schemes provided limited access to funds and limited investment
direction. There must be a genuine commercial reason for their establishment and they are subject to approval by the Superannuation Funds
Office, which usually permits up to 50 per cent of the accumulated
funds to be loaned back to or invested in the company.

Self-employment. Whether a person is self-employed or an employee
may be quite easy to see in some circumstances, but in others it may
be very difficult. The factors distinguishing an employment from
self-employment are many and varied: the basic principles behind any

decision is whether there is a contract of service (Schedule E) or a contract for services (Schedule D). The classic illustration (by Lord Denning) was to look at a ship's master, a chauffeur and a newspaper reporter, who are all employed under a contract of service as compared with a ship's pilot, a taxi-driver and a newspaper contributor, who work under a contract for services. (See TRADE.)

Lately the Revenue has been much less willing to admit self-employment where it could be argued that there was a master/servant relationship and from time to time reclassifies certain workers as employees when they might previously have been claiming the liberality of the Schedule D expenses rule. For example, film technicians were so reclassified in 1983 although the Revenue had less success with the North Sea DIVERS. Private Members' Bills appear on this subject in the House from time to time.

Self-employed retirement annuities. See RETIREMENT ANNUITY.

Seminars and conferences etc. Not generally taxable if the expenditure on them is borne and paid for by the employer, whether the employee is high or low paid, and provided the subjects of the lectures and discussions are directly related to the employment.

Separate assessment; separate taxation of wife's earnings; separation of spouses. See HUSBAND AND WIFE.

Settlement or trust. A trust arises where one person, the trustee, holds assets for the benefit of another person, or a class of persons (of whom he may be one), who are called the beneficiaries.

A trust may be created orally or in writing, during lifetime or on death. By whichever means the trust is created, however, it must satisfy three legal requirements, known as the *three certainties*:

(a) the words used to create the trust must be imperative;
(b) the subject matter of the gift must be certain;
(c) the persons, or class of persons, who are to benefit must be clear from the outset.

Trustees are required to make a return to the Inland Revenue setting out all income and capital gains which relate to trust property and they are responsible for paying any tax due. If income is accumulated or payable at the discretion of the trustees then they will be liable for basic rate income tax plus an additional tax at 16 per cent. In other cases, they will be liable for basic rate only.

Settlement after Inland Revenue investigation. After a Revenue investigation the settlement procedure has two final and separate features. First, the taxpayer agrees to pay the amount of the settlement payable by reason of his default in return for criminal proceedings not being taken against him; this amount is usually payable in one sum but it is possible to arrange instalments. Second, the taxpayer is requested to sign a CERTIFICATE OF FULL DISCLOSURE– that he has disclosed all his assets, all his sources of income and all facts bearing on his tax liability. If there is a later enquiry, the signing of such a certificate makes the possible penalty position much more serious.

Settlor. Defined as any person by whom the SETTLEMENT in question was made, being a person who has entered into the settlement directly or indirectly; in particular if he has provided funds directly or indirectly for the purpose of the settlement or has made, with any other person, a reciprocal arrangement for that other person to enter into the settlement.

Share incentive schemes. An arrangement whereby a person acquires shares or an interest in shares in a company in pursuance of a right granted to him as a director or employee of that company and not in pursuance of an offer to the public. The value of such a benefit is chargeable to tax under Schedule E as earned income; and after seven years on the excess of the market value then over the original acquisition price or the earlier disposal on the excess of the sale proceeds over original cost (with an adjustment for any amounts already charged to income tax).

There are a number of schemes that may be set up, with Revenue approval, to avoid these tax liabilities: see APPROVED SHARE OPTION SCHEMES, PROFIT SHARING SCHEMES, SAVINGS RELATED SHARE OPTION SCHEMES.

Shadow directors. In relation to a company the phrase means a person on whose directions or instructions the directors of the company are accustomed to act. However, a person is not deemed a shadow director by reason only that the directors act on advice given by him in a professional capacity. See DIRECTOR, NOMINEE DIRECTORS.

Sick pay. It has always been the practice to tax pay from an employer during sickness or other absence from work. After April 5, 1982, any payments of STATUTORY SICK PAY under the Social Security Act of that year made by the employer (and refunded by the DHSS) will also be taxable. From 1983/84 onwards any employed person assessable under Schedule E is liable under that Schedule on any sum paid to him or his dependants from any scheme entered into by his employer in respect of his absence from work through sickness, injury and so on. The only exceptions are sick pay arrangements made and paid for by employees. Advice on running sick pay schemes may be had from Inland Revenue, Technical Division, Room 59, New Wing, Somerset House, Strand, London WC2L 1LB. See SICKNESS BENEFIT below.

Sickness benefit. As stated under SICK PAY above, private sick pay arrangements are not normally taxable; however, if they continue for at least twelve months, they may become so.

Single person's allowance. See ALLOWANCES.

Six months. A criterion in considering whether a person is ORDINARILY RESIDENT in the UK. It has been held to comprise six calendar months with hours being taken into account, according to the courts. In practice, it is taken to comprise 183 days.

Small maintenance payments. Payments under a court order:

(a) by one of the parties to a marriage to or for the benefit of the other party to the marriage or for that other party's maintenance; or
(b) to any person under 18 for his own benefit, maintenance or education; or
(c) to any person for the benefit, maintenance or education of a person under 18 years of age.

No tax is deductible where payments do not exceed in (a) or (b) £33 per week or £143 per month and in (c) £18 per week or £78 per month currently; these limits are subject to regular review.

Social security benefits. Some of the long list of benefits are taxable and some are not. In the first category, the most common are pensions of all types, supplementary and unemployment benefit, invalid care allowance, invalidity allowance (paid with pension) and job release allowance paid earlier than one year before pensionable age. Not assessable, in broad outline, are means-tested benefits, industrial injury benefits, war disablement benefits including war widows' and war orphans' pensions. Other benefits which are not assessable include attendance allowance, child benefit, pensioners' Christmas bonus, death grant, employment rehabilitation allowance, invalidity allowance and pensions, job release benefit (within one year of pensionable age), job search and employment transfer scheme benefits, maternity grants, mobility allowance from 1982/83, student grants and job training and similar schemes allowances. Benefits and their taxability change from time to time (for example, mobility allowance) and the conditions should always be checked.

Solicitor.

(a) When a solicitor pays a client an amount in lieu of the interest which would have accrued if money had been deposited in a designated account, then that amount is assessable on the client.

(b) At an appeal meeting (see OBJECTIONS AND APPEALS) a solicitor is entitled to make a submission in writing, whereas an accountant must make his orally.

(c) A solicitor can be assessed under Schedule E in respect of an office, but if such an office is incidental to the practice, the emolument arising is usually as a matter of convenience included in his Schedule D, Case II computation. It will normally be necessary to request such a concession and it would not be available for, say, a recordership.

Somerset House. 1785 marked the occupation (not of course by force) of Somerset House by various public offices, in particular the Commissioners of Taxes and the Stamp Office. There has been a building on the site for over four centuries and it was originally the home of the Lord Protector Somerset in the 16th century; hence the name. Queen Elizabeth held her Council meetings there; Oliver Cromwell lay in state there, and it had been the home of the Stuart dowager queens. Towards the end of the 18th century it was decaying fast and Sir William Chambers was commissioned to develop the six acre site. By 1785 the east wing was taken over and it has been the home of the Inland Revenue ever since.

The portals facing the Strand used to have on each side the notice 'Dead Slow'. These have now been discreetly removed but whether this action is justified is open to question.

Special Commissioners. Created in 1805 to satisfy those táxpayers who did not fancy the thought of the local GENERAL COMMISSIONERS knowing about their tax affairs. From that modest beginning has developed the formidable battery of powers which they now deploy. They tend to hear the more complex, technical appeals and it is possible to transfer cases originally intended to be heard by General Commissioners to them for hearing. There are currently seven Commissioners, who are all qualified lawyers of at least ten years' standing; they hear appeals in the same way as the General Commissioners, but their procedure is more formal. They are paid a salary fixed by the Minister for the Civil Service, and normally sit in London at Turnstile House, 94–99 High Holborn, London WCN 6LQ. They do, however, hold hearings regularly in the principal cities of the UK. Only one Special Commissioner takes a hearing unless the Chairman of the Special Commissioners decides that the contentious point is of such importance that it requires two. They have published Notes on Appeals which can be obtained from the address above.

Special investigation section. A small unit stationed at Melbourne House, Aldwych with which only a very few taxpayers and their advisers would ever be concerned. The Section has always specialised in dealing with the most complicated of avoidance cases where matters of legislative interpretation are at issue as well as large sums of tax. Multinational corporations may be involved in such cases, many of which are decided in the Courts.

Special office. When IN-DEPTH INVESTIGATIONS were adopted as a Revenue policy, it was also realised that a new arm for investigation was needed which would not, like ENQUIRY BRANCH, simply concentrate on major fraud cases, but deal with activities where a lot of money was generated in a short period by, say, pop groups, or where receipts were high but so were expenses, as in the case of actors, or where wealthy people were claiming not to be residents (GHOSTS). Beginning in 1973, twelve Special Offices have been set up and they have turned out to be very cost effective. Although their Inspectors have no more power than Inspectors in Districts, they exercise it more aggressively, with the aim of achieving a satisfactory (to the Revenue) settlement.

Spread of receipts. A relief confined to authors of literary, dramatic, musical or artistic work for the whole or partial assignment of copyright; in 1983 it was extended to payments made under the public lending rights. When the consideration for the assignment is a lump sum then this can be spread over various periods according to the time he was engaged in the work which must have been more than twelve months. It is a further illustration of the advantage of Schedule D over Schedule E: a director who earns a large bonus or commission during a successful year has no such privilege.

Staff entertainment. There were cries of 'Scrooge' when the Revenue was known to be considering the allowability of such entertainment under Schedule D, Case I or the taxability as a benefit under Schedule E. However, a reasonable compromise was arrived at (see PARTIES).

Statements of practice. Since 1978 the Revenue has redesignated its more significant PRESS RELEASES as statements of practice and numbered them consecutively in the year of issue – for example, 6/78, 7/79, 10/80 and so on. Some of the pre-1978 press releases have also been issued as statements of practice. They are intended to enlarge on the

Revenue's interpretation and application of the legislation in practice, although they have no statutory force and do not necessarily bind taxpayers to follow them. There is an index, updated annually, obtainable from Inland Revenue, Public Enquiry Room, New Wing, Somerset House, Strand, London WC2R 1LB (a large stamped addressed envelope will be needed).

Statutory sick pay schemes. From April 6, 1983, the Social Security and Housing Benefits Act, 1982, provided for employers to make payments to employees who fall sick and to recover the tax from the DHSS. The Revenue will advise on the proportion of employer's contribution. There was a press release dated August 18, 1981, on the subject. These payments are subject to PAYE and national insurance contributions.

Statutory instrument. In general, when the power of subordinate legislation – that is, legislation elucidating points in a major statute – is conferred upon a minister, any document by which that power is exercised is known as a statutory instrument. It has the force of law, usually having lain on the table of the House of Commons for a prescribed period.

Street works. Relief on interest from allowable loans relating to a private residence includes any works for sewering, surfacing and generally making good a road. It even includes the lighting.

Students. In general, income arising from a scholarship held by a student receiving full-time instruction at an educational establishment is exempt from tax. The Board of Inland Revenue may consult the educational authorities concerned about the nature of such a scholarship. When a person who has been in full-time employment becomes a full-time scholar income up to £4,000 may be regarded as a grant and not taxed. Income above £4,000 is wholly taxed. Wages from holiday employment may be paid free of tax if the annual income does not exceed the exemption limit. The form P38(S) should be completed.

Subscriptions. Like membership of PROFESSIONAL BODIES, LEARNED SOCIETIES, when payment of subscriptions is a condition of the performance of the duties of the office and the sole or main activities of the body are relevant to the employment concerned then such payments are allowable. The general criteria for approving such a body are that it must be concerned with the spread of knowledge and the standards and protection of its members. Trade union subscriptions must also meet these requirements to be allowable. If the objects are not wholly met or directed otherwise, the Board of Inland Revenue may fix a proportion to be allowed. A list of approved subscriptions is published (for the address see PROFESSIONAL BODIES). However, approval of a subscription does not necessarily mean it will be allowed; that depends on the particular circumstances of the case.

Sub-contractors in the construction industry. See CONSTRUCTION INDUSTRY EMPLOYEES.

Sub-postmaster. This position is often combined with running a shop. It is customary to include the salary from the Post Office in the total receipts and to issue an NT (no tax) coding. This practice is extended to the situation in which a limited company operates a sub-post office. If the nominee director acting as sub-postmaster hands over his salary to the company then that is included in the trading profits and taxed to corporation tax.

Subsidiary source of income. One DISTRICT takes the responsibility of dealing with any one taxpayer's return, but it will not have knowledge of all subsidiary sources of income – such as, for instance, a second employment. So it is necessary first to verify the amount of the subsidiary income from the DISTRICT which deals with it and then instruct that DISTRICT how it is to be taxed. If it is not large, the taxpayer's coding may be adjusted and the amount 'coded out', which dispenses with the need to make a formal assessment. If this cannot be done or is otherwise not convenient, assessment instructions will be issued.

Subsistence allowance. Given when employees are temporarily working away from home and their normal place of employment. It is intended to cover the additional cost of food and travel when away on duty; no allowance can be made for these when employees are at their normal place of work. So long as the amount is reasonable, the Revenue will not normally seek to tax it.

Suggestions schemes. See AWARDS.

Superannuation. Payments to employees to approved superannuation schemes are allowed in the tax year in which they are paid. They are deducted from gross pay for PAYE purposes: this is known as the 'net pay arrangement' and was introduced in 1973; National Insurance Contributions, however, continue to be calculated on gross pay (see RETIREMENT and RETIREMENT ANNUITIES).

T

Tax accountant. The statutory definition is a person who assists another person in the preparation of returns or accounts to be made or delivered by that other person for any purpose of tax. The Revenue has the power to call for documents in his possession or power if they have sufficient cause. There is a penalty for assisting in, or inducing, the making or delivery of a return or accounts known to be incorrect. The maximum of such penalty is currently £500. A taxpayer cannot plead the neglect of an agent as an excuse for his own.

Tax cases. Tax law has two sources: statute law enacted by Parliament (see INCOME AND CORPORATION TAXES ACT, 1970 and TAXES MANAGE-MENT ACT, 1970), and case law established by the Courts. In 1874 the right to state a case for the opinion of the High Court was introduced and since that time 55 plus volumes of tax cases testify to the need of interpreting the words of the parliamentary draftsmen. Some decisions have had dramatic effects on tax problems. But it should be remembered that each case is decided on its own particular facts and generalising or quoting judicial pronouncements from them can be dangerous, apart from always keeping in mind one classic pronouncement to a lady appellant: 'If you go on spending your time on tax cases and the like, it will drive you silly.'

Tax credit. Defined as the proportion of the amount or value of a dividend paid by a company resident in the UK corresponding to the rate of advance corporation tax; this is the amount of corporation (that is, company) tax paid on its dividends by a company resident in the UK. As the tax credit is linked to the basic rate, basic rate taxpayers end up by paying no further tax on their dividends.

Tax credit relief. A person who has unused ALLOWANCES may claim the repayment of tax credits on dividends within six years of the end of the tax year for which the claim is made. Non-residents in the UK may also claim tax credit relief under DOUBLE TAXATION treaties.

Tax-free disability payment. Where a payment is made to an employee on leaving his employment because of a disability, there is generally no liability to tax. Disability is not only a condition resulting from a sudden affliction but also continuing incapacity to work because of deteriorating physical or mental health caused by chronic illness.

Tax-free remuneration. In practice there is no such thing. If an employer pays an employee a sum of money without operating PAYE and deducting tax, the payment is regarded as a net payment. To arrive at the measure of the remuneration it needs to be grossed up: that is, if the weekly payment was £140 and tax was 30 per cent, that amount would represent only 70 per cent of the taxable remuneration and would need to be grossed up by a fraction of $\frac{100}{70}$; so the true remuneration is £200. See also REGULATION 29.

Tax havens. A tax haven is a country, colony or area where the tax rates are substantially lower than those of most countries; they may even be nil. Individuals not resident in the UK may use them to shelter investment income, by means of offshore funds and companies by way of a dividend holding company. When nearness and political stability are important, most people in the UK think of the Channel Islands or the Isle of Man; these prefer, however, to be known as 'low tax areas' rather than be labelled 'tax havens' – a phrase which sometimes has dubious implications. *Controlled foreign companies* legislation needs to be considered in relation to their use.

Tax raids. What may seem to be a somewhat dramatic entry covers the fact that the Revenue (admittedly with safeguards) has more rights of entry and inspection than it used to have, although they still do not approach those of Customs and Excise. Perhaps the most spectacular use of the recent powers of entry granted to the Revenue in 1976 was the ROSSMINSTER raids on July 13, 1979, starting at 7 am. In fact, these powers are rarely used and if so, much more circumspectly.

Tax tables. Issued by the Revenue not only to employers but to accountants and libraries. They show the cumulative free pay for each weekly or monthly period in relation to each type of code. That amount is subtracted from the total gross pay up to that time leaving the amount of taxable pay on which the tax due (or refundable to) the employee is calculated. There is a modified system for employees on fixed wages, and there are 'prefix F' codes, which are non-cumulative.

Taxable income. Defined as the amount on which income tax is charged. It is the TOTAL INCOME of an individual in the year of assessment less his personal reliefs.

Taxes Management Act, 1970. The Taxes Management Act, 1970 and its supporting regulations, to give the full title, came into force for all purposes on April 6, 1970. It was, like the INCOME AND CORPORATION TAXES ACT, 1970, a consolidating Act. It is divided into twelve parts and four schedules and deals with administration, returns, assessments, collection, penalties and appeals. It is more neglected than it should be since it is the framework around which the administration and operation of our present tax system is constructed.

Teachers. There is now some relaxation in the statutorily restrictive EXPENSES rule. Travelling expenses may be claimed for out of school functions; a claim was always valid for supply teachers, and for certain expenses of teachers in polytechnics and colleges. But where a member of a religious teaching order applies the salary to that order an assessment is still raised on the recipient. See HEADTEACHERS.

Telephone charges. The rental of a telephone installed at the employer's behest has been held not to be allowable because it was not used wholly and exclusively in the performance of the duties; telephone charges have also been disallowed in the case of a consultant anaesthetist. Use for emergency purposes only might be considered and also where home is used as an office.

Terminal payments. See GOLDEN HANDSHAKE.

Theatrical and film employees. Acting in general has been held to be a profession; but where a performer is employed under a standard contract for a certain period and no outside work is stipulated then the correct schedule of charge is Schedule E.

No problem arises here since the Revenue issued guidelines listing grades of staff other than performers where assessment under Schedule D would be accepted. As far as part-time employees are concerned, the employer is under an obligation to operate PAYE where necessary and to keep records of names and addresses when payments are made gross on the understanding that the recipients are not liable to tax.

Time limits. It is useless to look for any uniformity, logic or consistency in time limits. There have been odd moves to regularise what has been described as a jungle, but there has never been a root and branch attempt at reform. A summary of the current position as far as Schedule E is concerned is as follows.

Thirty days for appeals against assessments, appeals to High Court (see OBJECTIONS AND APPEALS), delivery of RETURNS, payment of tax (usually within 30 days of the notice of assessment).

Three months for appeals against the Board's decisions on residence matters, application for judicial review (see PREROGATIVE ORDERS).

Twelve months. Notification of chargeability to tax must be given within one year after the end of the year of assessment, election or revocation for separate assessment of wife's earnings (see HUSBAND AND WIFE). Payment of retirement annuity premiums by an individual in non-pensionable employment must be made within one year of the end of the year of assessment in which they are to be claimed for relief.

Two years for a claim for rent to be assessed under Schedule A when furniture also supplied; absence on business abroad; Schedule D, Case III, IV and V election for cessation rules to apply in certain circumstances, for example, when no income arose during the last two years of possession.

Five years. Formal assessments may be made under Schedule E if the taxpayer gives notice within five years after the end of the year of assessment.

Six years for ERROR OR MISTAKE CLAIM; claim for further allowances omitted from return; claim against double assessment; double tax relief; relief for interest payable; delayed receipt of overseas remittances; unused retirement annuities relief; Schedule D, Cases III, IV and V claims for actual basis to apply when normally assessment on previous year, claims for cessation of source of income, claims generally.

In some cases the time limits may be extended at the discretion of the Revenue, but there should always be good and sufficient reason. Failure to claim in time should be remedied as soon as possible after the discovery of the omission.

Tips. It has been admitted (see GRATUITIES) that the twin elements of service and expectation make tips assessable for tax. From a practical point of view, while hotels and restaurants often operate a TRONC system, taxi-drivers, hairdressers and so on are often assessed on an estimated addition to receipts or wages for the elements of gratuity.

Tool allowance. There is a flat rate allowance for tools (see also CLOTHING) depending on the nature of the occupation. This does not, however, debar an individual from claiming the actual expenditure if it is more advantageous.

Top-slicing relief. Operates to reduce an individual's liability to income tax on payments received as compensation for loss of office, on a chargeable event (for example, on surrender of a non-qualifying life policy) or a premium under a lease. The computation for the first of these has been simplified; see COMPENSATION FOR LOSS OF OFFICE.

Total income. This has a statutory definition: all income whether taxed by assessment or by deduction of tax at source less any annual charges or interest paid, and less any unrelieved losses.

Trade. To define trading, whether or not a transaction or series of transactions amounts to a trade is a subject which is often before the Courts and out of their decisions have evolved the so-called 'badges of trade'. But it may be equally relevant in the context of whether the activity in question consists of a trade or an employment. The Revenue is known to consider with great care whether the particular circumstances of a case justify a claim to SELF-EMPLOYMENT. Whether or not a trade is being carried on can be self-evident, depending on the type of activity, premises, number of customers and so on. But there is an increasing number of activities where the dividing line between a trade and an employment is difficult to draw. It is often a good idea to discuss such a problem with the Revenue rather than to put the case in writing; if there is any immediate rule of thumb it is that a contract of service attracts Schedule E, a contract for services, Schedule D.

Traded option. Gives the right to buy or sell a particular share quoted on a recognised stock exchange at a specific price within a specified time period. Investors aim to profit by taking advantage of favourable changes in the share's market price. The option itself can be bought and sold, hence the significance of 'traded'.

Trade union. To be entitled to tax exemption trade unions must be registered. They are then entitled to exemption on income which is not trading income and is applied to provident benefits; these are limited in amount but include legal expenses in representing members at Industrial Tribunal hearings. The unions negotiate CLOTHING and TOOL allowances.

Transfer of assets abroad. An extremely complex subject and the legislation designed to counter elaborate avoidance schemes involving the transfer of assets is equally complex. The situation may arise when, first, an individual ORDINARILY RESIDENT in the UK transfers assets in such a way that he is entitled to receive a capital sum or can enjoy the income of a non-resident in the UK; second, by a similar transfer, income becomes payable to a person not resident in the UK; or third, a UK resident, who is not liable to tax under the legislation, receives a benefit out of assets through their transfer or any associated operation. In any of these three circumstances, if one of the purposes was the avoidance of taxation, the value of the benefit is treated as income of a person who is RESIDENT in the UK for all tax purposes and assessed under Schedule D, Case VI.

Transfer of value not at arm's length. MARKET VALUE is generally substituted where a transaction takes place other than AT ARM'S LENGTH.

Transport vouchers. Defined as any ticket, other document or pass intended to enable a person in possession of it to obtain some form of passenger transport services. For higher paid employees these always were taxable: for lower paid, such vouchers were not taxable subject to certain conditions: from April 6, 1982, they were made taxable. See also SEASON TICKETS.

Travelling expenses. To be allowable for Schedule E purposes, travelling expenses must be wholly, exclusively and necessarily incurred in the performance of the duties. This covers the travelling expenses of a representative who is travelling in the performance of his duties (see COMMERCIAL TRAVELLER). It also covers travel between two locations during the course of one employment. By concession, the expenses of travelling between different locations in the course of duties for other companies in the same group is normally allowable also. It does not cover travel from home to work since the duties do not start until the place of employment is reached and the travelling is therefore not in the course of those duties. But here again, the position can be modified if the employee is required to work from his own home and not his employer's place of business.

Travelling expenses from the main place of employment to the site of work are allowable when an employee is temporarily required to work away; the cost of additional travel from home to work if outside working hours may also be allowable. One last point: when the necessity of the travelling expenses has been established, the 'wholly and exclusively' element is not pressed if, for example, the employee has a night out before returning home.

These requirements are somewhat relaxed in relation to overseas travel to perform the duties of an employment outside the UK. See EXPENSES.

Troncs. A system whereby all the gratuities and service charges in a hotel, restaurant and so on are pooled and shared out among the staff, usually in proportion to their position. These amounts are, of course, emoluments and the person responsible for operating the tronc (the tronc master) is also responsible for operating the PAYE deductions, in effect as if he were the employer. See also GRATUITIES and TIPS.

Trusts. See SETTLEMENTS AND TRUSTS.

Trust income. The untaxed income of a trust assessable under Schedule A or Schedule D may be assessed on the trustee as the person entitled to receive it; but if he authorises its payment to the beneficiary direct, he will not then be assessed. A trustee may be required to make a return of the income chargeable on him but in practice trustees deliver an annual statement of income less expenses from which the liability is computed and the beneficiaries' share of the net trust income thus worked out. The income of *discretionary* and *accumulation* trusts is taxed at an additional rate of 16 per cent in addition to basic rate, unless the income is treated as that of the settlor or is exempt for charitable or other reasons; taxed overseas income will be entitled to the appropriate double tax relief. See SETTLEMENTS AND TRUSTS.

Trustee. When property is vested in or held by one person on behalf of and for the benefit of another, the first is the trustee and the second is the beneficiary. A trustee is therefore any person in whom the settled property or its management is, for the time being, vested. Trustees are also needed for approved PROFIT SHARING SCHEMES. See SETTLEMENTS AND TRUSTS.

U

Underlying tax. Term met when considering DOUBLE TAXATION RELIEF. It refers to tax charged against the profits of an overseas company before a dividend is paid; it therefore does not represent tax directly charged in relation to the dividend.

Underpayment. From an administrative standpoint, underpayment procedure by the Revenue is very elaborate, covering nearly two pages of indexations. Fortunately for the taxpayer, the practical position is more simple. If the Revenue makes an assessment which reveals an underpayment, this is automatically repaid. If an individual considers tax has been over-deducted during the year, then an assessment should be requested. See ASSESSMENT.

Underwriters. There are special provisions for assessing underwriters, which were amended in 1973. The basic principle is that assessments are made on the current year basis.

Underwriting is, of course, principally associated with Names at Lloyd's. There are more than 24,000 Names and the minimum capital requirement is £100,000. A Name is considered to be carrying on a business through a permanent establishment in the UK, and the income and gains arising from membership are assessed for the tax year to April 5 in which the calendar year account ends – in other words, the income and gains for the 1986 account are assessed in 1986/87. These profits or gains consist of the underwriting profit or loss, the interest and dividends on invested premiums and capital gains. Dividends and interest on the personal investments deposited with Lloyd's and so on are returned by the Name on his personal return. The tax liability can be mitigated to a limited extent by transferring cash and investments into a Lloyd's Special Reserve Fund. Relief is available for losses, tax credits and certain expenses. This is only a very brief review of a subject so complex that the Revenue has now centralised all work in connection with Lloyd's underwriters in a special District in London and a specialist unit in Shipley.

Unemployment benefit. Since July 4, 1982, the Department of Employment holds records of a claimant's tax history. At the end of the claimant's period of benefit claim (if earlier, at the end of the tax year) his tax position is calculated by the Department and notified to the claimant and the Revenue. Any dispute regarding the amount of the taxable benefit, which is computed by a 'benefits officer', is referred to the GENERAL COMMISSIONERS. The time limit is 60 days for such an appeal.

Unilateral relief. Limited relief is provided from UK income tax and corporation tax by way of credit for tax payable under the law of any territory outside the UK where there is no specific double tax treaty between that territory and the UK. See DOUBLE TAXATION.

University teachers. No tax problem normally arises on their university or college salary which will be subject to PAYE; their coding will also be applied to any lecture fees. As far as private tuition is concerned, that would be a separate venture and assessable either under Schedule D, Case VI or Case II depending on the amount and regularity of the receipts as well as the organisation of the activity. Conference expenses and subscriptions are dealt with in accordance with standard Schedule E rules and practice. See TEACHERS.

Unearned income. Sometimes referred to as investment income; an alternative simple definition is any income which is not earned. It includes annual payments such as annuities, income from deeds of covenant and maintenance, building society and bank interest, dividends of all kinds, and rents unless the letting amounts to a trade (see FURNISHED LETTING).

Unpaid remuneration at April 5. When this is assessed (see ASSESSMENT) it may throw up a 'notional underpayment'. This will normally be taken into account in a subsequent tax year when the amount is paid. A concessional repayment may be made in certain cases where there is also an overpayment of tax arising because of insufficient allowances having been given in the PAYE coding for the year.

Unremittable overseas income. Where overseas income assessable on an arising basis cannot be transferred to the UK either because of the laws of the territory in which the income arises or by an executive act of its governments or because it is impossible to obtain the necessary foreign exchange; then the individual entitled to that income will not be charged to tax in respect of it until such time as he is *able* to arrange the remittance of such income to the UK (irrespective of whether he does so or not).

Unused relief. Refers to RETIREMENT ANNUITIES (it was also used in connection with stock relief before that was abolished). Any relief available for a year of assessment which is not used in that year may be carried forward and can then be set against qualifying premiums paid in any of the next six years. Relief is granted for the year in which the premium is paid but the maximum relief for that year must be used in priority and unused relief for earlier years must be used before the unused relief which has arisen in later years.

When an assessment becomes final and conclusive more than six years after the end of the year of assessment to which it relates – at the end, say, of an investigation settlement – and results in unused relief, that amount is not available for any of the six following years; but it can be franked by a qualifying premium paid within six months of the date on which the assessment becomes final and conclusive, provided the maximum premium allowable for that year is paid.

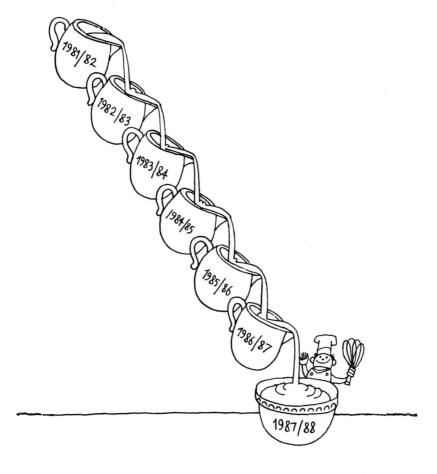

V

VAT deregistration. A registered trader (see VAT REGISTRATION) whose taxable supplies fall below certain limits may apply to be deregistered. Traders are entitled to apply if they have been registered for two years and their taxable supplies in both years have been below the registration limit (currently £20,500) or at any time if CUSTOMS AND EXCISE accepts that in the coming year taxable supplies will fall below a certain limit (currently £19,500).

VAT registration. A trader who makes taxable supplies which exceed the registration limits must register for VAT; if he does not, then VAT will be payable even though it has not been charged to customers. The limits in question are currently £7,000 for any quarter, £20,500 for any four quarters or a reasonable belief that the £20,500 limit will be exceeded in the next four quarters. There are penalties for failure to register.

VAT and Schedule E. For PAYE purposes, VAT is excluded from payments for services supplied by a person holding an office or employment but benefits and any other expenses chargeable on an employee should include VAT, if any.

Vocation. Defined as a calling (which is its Latin derivation) and means the way in which a person passes his life. Some rather materialistic occupations have been held to be vocations – those of a bookmaker, a jockey and a land agent, for instance – as well as the more imaginative pursuits of author or actor. From a tax point of view vocations and professions are given the same treatment. Until 1922 it was not necessary to draw any distinction between professions, employments and vocations; but when by the Finance Act of that year employments were transferred to Schedule E the distinction became important. (See SELF-EMPLOYMENT and TRADE.)

Voluntary allowance. A phrase relevant, for instance, in the requirement for the higher personal allowance (see ALLOWANCES) which is due when the wife is wholly maintained voluntarily by her husband although they may not be living together; such an allowance is not assessable on the recipient. But voluntary payments by an employer will be assessable if for services as are also voluntary pensions.

Vouchers. A catch-all term which covers both cash and non-cash vouchers. A CASH VOUCHER is any sort of document which can be exchanged for cash equal to, greater or not substantially less than the cost to the person providing it. A NON-CASH VOUCHER is one which cannot be exchanged for cash but which provides money's worth in the shape of goods or services: it also includes a cheque voucher which an employee may use to pay for goods and services. All are deemed to be taxable emoluments, as are CREDIT CARDS, which are a form of voucher, and TRANSPORT VOUCHERS. See also BENEFIT, LUNCHEON VOUCHERS, SEASON TICKETS.

W

Waiter. See TIPS.

Waiver of remuneration. When the holder of an office (most commonly, a director) voluntarily surrenders part or the whole of his salary or bonus, then the question arises of what the quantum of his Schedule E assessment should be. In general, a mere waiver does not necessarily reduce the Schedule E assessment if, in the first place, the emoluments, whatever their nature, were put at his disposal. On the other hand, it has been held that where there was no intention that remuneration should ever be paid, then taxable emoluments did not arise. But if emoluments are received and handed over to a third party then the receipt of the emoluments in the first place is regarded as the decisive factor; this happened in the case of a professed nun who handed over her teacher's salary, as she was bound, to her Order; she was held to be correctly assessed to Schedule E on its original receipt.

A common situation is where remuneration is credited to a loan account but remains undrawn: even so, the remuneration is assessable when credited since there still remains a right to withdraw. Lastly, even if directors' remuneration is disallowed for corporation tax purposes, theoretically the whole still stays assessable on the director or directors concerned: it will not be assessed, however, if the amount is both formally waived *and* refunded to the company. (Incidentally, such remuneration does not rank as a distribution.)

War widows' pension. From 1979/80 pensions paid to widows in respect of death due to service in the armed forces – including wartime service in the merchant navy – and war injuries are exempt from tax. This exemption also covers similar payments made by governments outside the UK, and any other pension replacing one already exempt or partially so. See SOCIAL SECURITY PAYMENTS.

Wear and tear. See CAPITAL ALLOWANCES. The old term for depreciation to be allowed against profits, for which the new term capital allowance was substituted in 1945.

Week 1 and Month 1 tables. As explained under PAYE, the PAYE system normally works on a cumulative basis. However, there are special tables which set out the weekly or monthly proportion of an individual's allowances against his actual weekly or monthly earnings. Such tables should only be used where authorised by the PAYE regulations or by the INSPECTOR OF TAXES. This might be required when a decrease in code during the year might cause hardship because of the reduced net pay left after cumulative under-deductions. The underpayment at the end of the year would be taken into account in a subsequent coding and thus spread. The tables are also used for payments to a former employee which cannot be calculated before leaving, or when a new employee is unable to provide details of his pay and tax deducted at his previous employment. These tables may also be needed in cases of emergency codings if the P2 (coding notice) so specifies.

Week 53. As PAYE tables provide for the annual tax allowances to be allocated on a year of 52 weeks, where 53 pay days fall in any year the tax for the 53rd week is computed by reference to WEEK 1 TABLES.

Welfare, sports and social facilities. The benefit from these facilities is not taxable on lower paid employees since they are not convertible into cash; by concession they are not taxable on directors or higher paid employees either. The same considerations also apply to the benefits which may flow from the employer's contribution to hospitals, clinics and charities generally, but not to medical expenses in general (see MEDICAL INSURANCE).

Wales. Tax provisions are enacted and administered so as to have the same effect in England, Scotland, Wales and Northern Ireland (and in the Scilly Isles since 1954/55). Wales, however, is distinguished by having an income tax return worded in Welsh. When this was first introduced one fervent Welsh Nationalist was heard to complain that it was not in the correct dialect – presumably his.

Wholly and exclusively. A quotation from one of the sections dealing with the allowability of deductions for Schedule D purposes, and this phrase has been the subject of judicial interpretation ever since the stated case procedure was introduced in 1874. One of the vexed questions arising from it which has never been satisfactorily resolved is that of duality: strictly it means that if an expense is incurred both for business and for private purposes it cannot be said to be incurred 'exclusively' for business purposes and therefore should be disallowed altogether. In practice, if the expense can be reasonably apportioned between business and private, the Revenue will normally accept a deduction for the business element.

Here it should be underlined that the adverb 'necessarily' is *not* a condition for Schedule D deductibility but is an essential part of the Schedule E rule (see below).

Wholly, exclusively and necessarily. For expenditure to be allowed for Schedule E purposes, it must be incurred 'wholly, exclusively and necessarily' in the performance of the duties. The use of the preposition 'in' is as important as the three preceding adverbs since it cuts out immediately travel from home to place of work which cannot be in the performance of the duties since they do not begin until the place of work is reached (see TRAVELLING EXPENSES). As already mentioned above, 'wholly and exclusively' appear stringent but an allowance is not always disallowable when the total involved does not qualify – for instance, for the use of a room in a private house. The rule of thumb is whether it is possible to tease out the business strands from the total expenditure. In the case of a suit used partly for business and, inevitably, partly privately, it was held that this was not possible: the distinction between a suit worn all day and protective clothing is clear (see CLOTHING).

As far as 'necessarily' is concerned, the test is whether the duties can be performed without incurring the expenditure. The Revenue will not always agree that expenditure is necessary, even if authorised by the employer. Expenditure which merely helps an employee to perform his duties or enables him to perform them more efficiently is not deductible on this ground, and this interpretation has been upheld many times by the Courts.

Some expenses are specifically allowed by statute (see EXPENSES) such as SUPERANNUATION PAYMENTS, SUBSCRIPTIONS, CAPITAL ALLOWANCES (and interest on loans in connection with them), FLAT RATE EXPENSES, TRAVELLING and SUBSISTENCE EXPENSES. ROUND SUM ALLOWANCES are not looked upon with favour by the Revenue, always questioned and often disallowed. Note that cases involving expenses are still being heard by the COMMISSIONERS and the Courts, especially on the question of benefits which the Revenue is looking at carefully through the agency of SPECIAL OFFICE and AUDIT (PAYE).

Widows; wife's earned income allowance; wife's earnings election. See HUSBAND AND WIFE.

Wilful default. There is no statutory definition of wilful default. It is generally taken to mean a failure to do what is reasonable in the circumstances where the person knew exactly what he was doing, here 'wilful' is used in the sense of 'reckless'. It has been held to include the concealment of a bank account without adequate explanation; delays in the payment of tax; omission of profits and other sources of income on more than one occasion; and the acceptance of an assessment which the taxpayer knew was inadequate. The importance of wilful default is twofold. It justifies extended time limit assessments (that is, beyond the normal six year time limit) but the onus of proof is on the Revenue and the taxpayer does not have to prove himself innocent unless the Revenue produces adequate evidence to support the charge. See also FRAUD and NEGLECT. A category of 'neglect tinged with wilful default' has also been suggested, but this has been held to be closer to neglect than to default.

Wills. A will is defined as a testamentary disposition by which all the property which the person is free to dispose of passes to other people in accordance with its terms. The provisions of any will should be reviewed from time to time in accordance with current tax legislation; for instance, the INHERITANCE TAX premiums contained in the 1986 Finance Act may affect the terms of many wills. The three main characteristics of a will are: that is takes effect on death but not before; that it may be revoked at any time; and that it can deal with property acquired after it was made but before death.

Withholding tax. Where a resident of the UK receives a dividend from a non-resident company, a withholding tax, at a net rate on the amount of the dividend paid, is often deducted in the country of origin. This will be available for credit against the corresponding liability to UK tax on the dividend. See DOUBLE TAX RELIEF, UNDERLYING TAX.

Woodlands. Tax is charged under SCHEDULE B in respect of the occupation of woodlands if managed on a commercial basis and with a view to the realisation of profits. It follows that amenity woodlands are not taxed. The tax is charged on the occupier on one third of the annual value in the chargeable period. This annual value is based on the rack rental of the land in its natural and unimproved state, and rates as earned income. No capital allowances are granted and the Revenue has no claim for actual income over assessed value. The reason for this apparently preferential value is that the period taken for a tree to mature makes a proper assessment almost impossible: a typical timber area can take nearly 60 years from planting to felling.

It is possible to elect for assessment under Schedule D, Case I but such an election does not mean the occupier is carrying on a trade: specific mention therefore has to be made to give relief for losses, although this does not extend to carry back: capital allowances are, however, due.

Woodlands are now an extremely live issue for tax planners and there are many tax effective schemes available. (See also SCHEDULE B.)

Y

Year. The year 1986/87 means the YEAR OF ASSESSMENT beginning on April 6, 1986, and ending April 5, 1987. Any corresponding expression where two years are similarly placed means the year of assessment beginning on April 6 in the first of those years and ending on April 5 in the second. The 'financial year', however, means the twelve months ending on March 31 in matters relating to corporation tax or government finance.

Year of assessment. This means, with reference to any income tax, the YEAR for which such tax was imposed by any Act imposing income tax.

Yearly interest. The definition of yearly interest has been held to require the satisfaction of the following conditions for a loan.

(a) It must be a short loan.
(b) It must have a measure of permanence.
(c) It must be in the nature of an investment.
(d) It must not be repayable on demand.
(e) It must have a tract of future time.

Yearly interest can include interest not actually paid for a year if it is calculated on periods of not less than a year and is capable of continuing for at least a year.

Youth Training Schemes. There are a number of schemes sponsored by the government through the Manpower Services Commission, which itself has two divisions, one concerned with employment and the other with training. The Youth Training Scheme is designed to give a full year's skill training to school leavers of 16 or 17 years old (and disabled persons under 21). It is mainly a replacement of the Youth Opportunities Programme. From April 1986 it is being progressively extended to cover a two year programme. A trainee receives a tax-free weekly allowance; an employee will receive a wage as agreed under a contract of employment. This will be taxable if it exceeds the tax threshold; it must be at least equal to the trainee allowance. Grants are made to sponsors who take on unemployed people.

As far as adult schemes are concerned, the Job Training Scheme has replaced the old Training Opportunities Scheme (TOPS). The cost of training is free and the weekly training allowance, plus any additional allowances, is also tax free.

Inland Revenue explanatory pamphlets

The following pamphlets, obtainable free of charge from any tax district, may be found useful by a Schedule E taxpayer.

IR 4	Income tax and pensioners
IR 4 A	Age allowance
IR 6	Double taxation relief
IR 11	Tax treatment of interest paid
IR 12	Occupational pension schemes
IR 13	Wife's earnings election
IR 14/15	Construction industry tax deduction scheme
IR 20	Residents and non-residents
IR 21	Tax tables
IR 22	Personal allowances
IR 23	Widows
IR 24	Class 4 national insurance contributions
IR 27	Taxation of real property
IR 28	Starting in business
IR 29	One-parent families
IR 30	Separation and divorce
IR 31	Married couples
IR 32	Separate assessment
IR 33	School leavers
IR 34	PAYE
IR 35	Profit-sharing
IR 36	Approved profit-sharing schemes
IR 38	SAYE share options
IR 39	Approved savings-related share option schemes
IR 40	Conditions for getting a sub-contractor's tax certificate
IR 41	The unemployed
IR 42	Lay-offs and short-time work
IR 43	Strikes
IR 45	What happens when someone dies?
IR 47	Deeds of covenant by parent to adult student
IR 51	Business expansion scheme
IR 52	Your tax office
IR 53	PAYE for employers – thinking of taking someone on
IR 55	Bank interest: paying tax
IR 56	Employed or self-employed
CGT 4	Capital gains tax – owner-occupied houses
Miras 6	Mortgage interest and your tax relief
46 Q	Returning payments in the entertaining industry
480	Notes on expenses and benefits
P 7	Employer's guide to PAYE